Succeeding
as a
Documentary
Filmmaker

Succeeding as a Documentary Filmmaker

A Guide to the Professional World

Alan Rosenthal

Southern Illinois University Press
Carbondale and Edwardsville

14 13 12 11   4 3 2 1

Library of Congress Cataloging-in-Publication Data
Rosenthal, Alan, [date]
Succeeding as a documentary filmmaker : a guide to
the professional world / Alan Rosenthal.
     p. cm.
Includes bibliographical references and index.
ISBN-13: 978-0-8093-3033-1 (pbk. : alk. paper)
ISBN-10: 0-8093-3033-4 (pbk. : alk. paper)
ISBN-13: 978-0-8093-8634-5 (ebook)
ISBN-10: 0-8093-8634-8 (ebook)
1. Documentary films—Production and direction.
I. Title.
PN1995.9.D6R645 2011
070.1'8—dc22   2010028848

Printed on recycled paper. ♻

The paper used in this publication meets the minimum requirements of American National Standard
for Information Sciences—Permanence of Paper for
Printed Library Materials, ANSI Z39.48-1992. ∞

For Beverly and David . . .
for all their help over so many years

Contents

Preface

MANY YEARS AGO, I WROTE that I distrust how-to books, whether about sex, how to make a million, or how to write that best-selling script. My attitude hasn't changed. This is not a how-to book but a guide to areas of documentary you may not be familiar with. As such, it deals with topics and subjects knowledge of which are absolutely essential if you are to succeed in the professional world of filmmakers.

Except in my brief afterword, I have said little about the goals or raison d'être of documentary. Yet, understanding those aims and purposes is absolutely essential, and at some time, you will have to address those questions very seriously. For me, working in documentary implies one is not just passively passing through this world but wants to change it for the better.

Many friends and also people I hardly knew assisted with this book. They sat down with me, drank endless cups of coffee with me, offered many suggestions, and replied with endless patience to my never-ending e-mails. My debt to them is enormous, and I hope I've included them all in the list below. If not, I beg their forgiveness. So my enormous thanks to: Mark Becker, Mark Benjamin, Mitch Block, Henry Breitrose, Jim Brown, Katie Cadigan, Gipsy Chang, Kevin Dawson, Nicole Draper, Jon Else, John Fox, Ron Frank, Veronica Fury, Helen Gaynor, Noit Geva, Gary Gladman, Peter Gottschalk, Mark Harris, Joost Hunningher, Judy Irving, Gabor Kalman, Faramarz K-Rahber, Jan Krawitz, Jerry Kuehl, Ian Lang, Melinda Levin, Jennifer Machiorlatti, John Marshall, Minda Martin, Sue Maslin, Len McClure, Carla Mertez, Shaun Miller, Michele Ohayon, Toni Perrine, Anika Pilnei, Russell Porter, Nenad Puhovski, Michael Rabiger, Pola Rapaport, Lilly Rivlin, Beverly Shaffer, Mort Silverstein, Robert Stone, Donald Taylor Black, Antony Thomas, Steve Thomas, Suree Towfighnia, Storry Walton, Leslie Woodhead, Pam Yates, and Tom

Zubrycki. Again, along with thanks, I acknowledge that all the discussion extracts I've used retain the copyright of the original writers.

I also thank Ben Levin and Ned Eckhardt, who read the draft manuscript and made many very helpful and creative suggestions for its improvement.

This is my fourth book for the Southern Illinois University Press, and, as usual, the Press has been a tremendous arm of support. Here my thanks go in particular to my editor Karl Kageff, who encouraged me from the first and made so many positive suggestions along the way. Finally, I express my gratitude to my copy editor, Mary Lou Kowaleski, and to Tirtza Rosenthal, who, as usual, was always there for me.

Succeeding
as a
Documentary
Filmmaker

1. Overview: The Route to Success

CAN YOU EARN A LIVING making documentary films? The answer is "yes." The aim of this book is to show how that goal can be achieved.

I didn't always think so positively. Often I would meet with new documentary students and ask them, "Who here is mad, crazy, nuts, and certifiably insane?" They would look at each other in wonder. Is this nonsensical rubbish what they'd paid $35,000 in tuition fees to hear? Then a few would get it and slowly raise their the hands. And those were the people I used to take as students because they had realized that as documentary filmmakers, they'd soon be poor, divorced, and bankrupt.

Well, I no longer think that way. I think changing conditions have made it much easier for the documentary filmmaker to make some decent money from his or her efforts. But to do that, students have to really understand what's happening in the marketplace and in television. This book, then, is meant to be the documentary filmmaker's guide to the real world, the world outside film school. It is intended to provide novices, students, graduate students, and current practitioners with the necessary know-how and skills to get ahead in the competitive and confusing world of professional documentary production.

In short, it's "The Lonely Planet" for all makers of documentary.

In a very down-to-earth way, this book introduces you to the commercial possibilities open to filmmakers and shows a variety of paths that will hopefully leave some money in your pocket at the end of the day. Inter alia, it discusses markets, finance, contracts, coproductions, and distribution, offering the hope that if the advice is followed, then documentary filmmaking might be a pretty good career path. And who knows, you might even be able to repay your parents for their help.

Changing Conditions

Recently, a Texas student told me he'd appeared with his film at various universities, sold two thousand DVDs, and arranged screenings on a few cable stations. More triumphantly he mentioned that he'd made about $15,000 profit after paying off all costs. This success would have been almost impossible twenty years ago and is mainly due to changing conditions in the industry. The student understood that and took advantage of the changes. To get ahead, you need to evaluate and understand those changing conditions.

Unfortunately, not all the changes are positive. At one time, the three major U.S. commercial networks screened about five hundred documentaries a year. Today, they barely make it into double figures—opportunities to work in and around the networks have virtually disappeared. However, the positive changes have more than offset those drawbacks.

The rise of cable TV, with specialist documentary outlets such as Discovery, National Geographic, A&E, and HBO, among others, all point to new opportunities. Equipment and film costs have drastically lowered, making it much easier and much more feasible for the filmmaker to get his or her own individual productions off the ground. The DVD has taken over the world, and new sales markets have opened up, including Amazon and the Internet. There has been a rise in coproductions and in the making of company and public-relations films. There has been an increasing demand for film graduates in industry. More documentaries are being shown in theaters, while more and more foundations have tuned in to financing nonfiction films. Film markets have become popular, and there has been a rise in film festivals and pitching opportunities to place films. Last but not least, I suspect that the demand for "reality" films will diminish, while the hunger for documentaries will increase.

This book will take you through all these changes and discuss their implications for your career advancement.

Know Your Objectives

I have a filmmaker friend Jane. Every few years, she makes an impassioned feminist tract or does a film about an obscure Balkan poet that rarely finds an audience above a few goats and old blind shepherds. OK. I'm making the last bit up. The point is she knows she cannot achieve anything above a minority audience. Yet Jane longs for commercial fame, wants to dress well, and buy quality jewelry. It seems to me that Jane fails to understand that her desire for impassioned minority filmmaking usually runs counter to her financial desires. She has in fact never sorted out her imperatives. She has never clearly laid down her career goals.

I suggest laying down your career goals is something worthwhile doing if you want to succeed. Try to sort through your goals and objectives. Try to figure out where you want to be and what you want to be doing in a few years. These goals and these objectives may well change with time, but it's worthwhile giving them a few minutes' thought when you start to go solo.

You think you know yourself, but do you really? Are you most comfortable working for others, or do you want to go into business for yourself? Is money important to you? Do you want to make politically impassioned films that will change the world? Or do you just enjoy filmmaking and are willing to try any subject?

Everyone has different objectives, and that's absolutely fine. All I'm saying is define what you want, and this book can help you to get there. The point is that you should be happy, really happy in what you do . . . and you should also be able to make a living.

Origins and Methods

This book arose out of a series of documentary workshops I conducted in Melbourne, Australia. My students came from all over the world; maybe half were Americans. One day, the conversation turned to film schools and what the students thought about their teachers, training, and courses. What almost everyone complained of was that while their schools talked ad nauseum about the road to Hollywood and features, discussion of documentary as a career was given very short shrift. It was scorned and laughed at. When faculty focused their students' eyes on an office on Hollywood and Vine and the half-million-dollar feature-writing contract, who had time to bother about poor documentary filmmakers?

Following that discussion, I thought about how the film-school attitude was reflected in the bookstores. What was easy to see was a plethora of books explaining how to make it in Hollywood, cozy up to Steven Spielberg, or find an agent in the best bars. The feature-bound student is inundated with advice. By contrast, it was clear to me that the documentary student was and is very poorly served, and what books there are have little or nothing to say about the professional path for nonfiction filmmakers.

Over the weeks, my discussions with the students gradually widened. Yes, the students all agreed, they had indeed learned some film skills at college. They knew all about equipment, which was great. But almost to a man or woman, they complained that their schools and departments had no vision of life after graduation . . . and they wanted some guidance.

These discussions kept reverberating in my mind for some time. I knew documentary could be fulfilling both as a life and as a professional career. And I knew, as I've mentioned, that external factors were improving for documentary filmmakers. Gradually the idea for this book was born. I would write a simple, short book showing how one could get on and move ahead in the post-film-school real world. Bingo! It was that simple.

I know my own limits. I've had a wide experience of filmmaking but wanted to go further. I decided I would ask a few friends, mostly mainstream professionals, how they started and got on in documentary. I would ask them for hints, suggestions for beginning filmmakers, secrets of the trade, all and any advice that would kick-start careers. And I would incorporate all this into the book. Well, I started off with a list of ten friends. I finished by hearing from over forty. That's the way it goes. You're thirsty, you open the tap, and suddenly your cup runneth over.

Book Progression

This book follows a fairly simple progression. It starts with the challenge of film or video training and concludes with a very full analysis of marketing and sales. You can work through the book progressively or dip into isolated chapters that may help you with current problems or work challenges.

After discussing how to make the most of film school and the acquisition of general skills in chapter 2, the next few sections help and advise you on how to take the first steps in what I call the real world. The purpose of chapters 5 and 6 are to help you clarify your options. These are basically whether to work for others or take the challenging route of the independent filmmaker. The following portions of the book, chapters 7 to 12, deal with basic survival knowledge. Here we discuss in detail the vital areas usually ignored by film schools, such as professional proposal writing, finance, going for grants, budgeting, contracts, pitching, and markets. The last part of the book, and maybe the most important, shows you how to maximize distribution and sales once the film is finished.

Here and there, but not very often, I've used short quotes or examples that have appeared in some earlier books of mine but that seem to me worthwhile repeating.

Generally, where I've referred to and named certain magazines, companies, or organizations that I think might be helpful to you, I have not included their dot.com references. The reason is that these change quite frequently, and it is child's play to look up the correct reference on Google.

As you work through the chapters, you'll see I've made one or two policy decisions. The first concerns the subject of video and film. This book is intended for both video and filmmakers. Some clients will want you to deliver on film, some on video. The basic commercial knowledge for creating both is almost identical.

The book also addresses documentary filmmaking and other forms of nonfiction film such as industrial, public relations, travel, teaching, and educational films. As a filmmaker who wants to survive financially, you may not be able to afford to pick and choose. Later on, you may have the luxury of saying, "I only want to make pure documentaries," but in the beginning, you'll probably try your hand at everything.

As you'll quickly see, this book is not about the *art* of filmmaking, so, generally, it doesn't discuss documentary directing, interviewing, or narration writing. I've assumed you have these skills. If not or you want to delve further into directing, you may want to glance at an earlier book of mine *Writing, Directing, and Producing Documentary Films and Videos.* Inter alia, that book discusses why we may want to make documentaries and the possible social goals of the filmmaker. These are very important issues, vital issues. They are the issues that made you choose this strange filmmaking path but are outside the scope of this current book. Here the main question is how to maximize your financial returns after the massive amount of work you've put into your films. A friend of mine once expressed it this way to me, and it's an observation I continually return to: "The successful filmmaker has his head full of dreams, his eyes on the mountains, but his feet are on the ground." Remember that, and you can't go wrong.

2. Making the Most of Film School

ONCE, IT WAS TRENDY TO be an art student. If you were a male student, the thing was to appear in a long, black coat, sport a fifteen-foot-long, red scarf, wear a beret, and smoke a pipe. For women, fish-net stockings helped, along with an assortment of peasant blouses culled from grandmother's bottom drawer or an elegant secondhand boutique on Manhattan's upper East Side. It was also vital that your fingers be stained and that you moved with a certain lassitude and insouciance that gave a hint of the cellars and ateliers of Montparnasse and beyond.

That is all passé. Today the vital thing is to be a film student. While denims and running shoes are necessary for both sexes, dress can vary from T-shirts to dress shirts and ties. The vital thing is to carry your film tripod with a swagger. You have to let the world know you're a film student, not a plodding law or accountancy nerd, and you're bound for fame and fortune in Hollywood and beyond.

Film schools or universities, colleges, and departments that include film in their curricula represent a growth industry. Pity the country that doesn't have its own national film school! In the United States, over a hundred institutions of higher learning provide courses in film and filmmaking. Australia, a huge country with a small population has over twenty state-university providers of film. Singapore, with less than five million inhabitants, boasts of over ten centers teaching professional filmmaking.

In the old days, there was only one or two serious ways to enter the film profession, by junior work in a film or TV studio or apprenticeship in a film house. Today, with fingers beckoning from everywhere, doors wide open, and advertisements assaulting prospective students from every magazine, it's easier than ever to go to film (and television) programs throughout the world. But are the time, effort, and expense well spent and worth it?

The Benefits of a Documentary Program

The first and key benefit of a good school is that it can provide you with technical skills in photography, editing, writing, and directing that are difficult, but not impossible, to master alone. Yes, with your PD 100 and your Final Cut Pro, you can go out and shoot your own films. It is much better in the long run, however, if someone teaches you how to master these tools in depth and use them with some art, craft, and skill. A good program should do exactly that. Furthermore, the good department can provide you with a wide variety of film equipment to play around with so that you experience all different kinds of editing machines and can handle 16 mm and 35 mm cameras as well as their low-cost video brothers and sisters.

An offshoot of all this is the chance to learn composite filmmaking. Of necessity, during the two or three years in the department, you'll be pushed into working on a variety of films, some standard, some experimental, and undertaking multiple tasks. One day, you'll act as cameraperson, the next as editor, while the following week you'll do sound or be asked to write a script. This is all to the good.

The process also teaches survival skills. Often, in an underequipped program, you have to battle for a camera, plead for extra editing time, or argue the case why your film should be chosen for production instead of that of another student's. Sounds terrible, doesn't it, but you might as well learn early that survival in the industry isn't for the meek and the mild but for those with strength, passion, and fire in the belly.

Outside of giving you technical skills and allowing you to familiarize yourself with the tools of the trade, the best film departments (and from now, I use this to include TV studies as well) can and should give an excellent media education. This means they instruct thoroughly in the way media works. They teach about the nature of broadcasting and industry structures in film and TV, both locally and throughout the world. This wider view can be of immense help in understanding the world after film school.

Film Departments and Documentary

Where the film department concentrates on documentary as a serious element of its program, there are multiple benefits. These include courses in documentary history and current documentary practices and the chance to meet with and listen to visiting filmmakers.

Learning about documentary history is not just an optional way to pass the time but is vital for anyone who seriously wants to be a documentary filmmaker. Such a course shows the wide options and practices in the field and stops you reinventing the wheel. Secondly, like a good art course, it shows you the best of the past in order to provoke you in the future. Thirdly, such a course helps you to define the boundaries between feature and documentary filmmaking and to understand why political and social criticism is such a vital part of documentary.

I mentioned the necessity for visiting filmmakers who do more than tell war stories. Why do we want them? Because the best of them provide inspiration and bring the real world into the film school. When they give screenings and explain their work, conduct pitching sessions, undertake master classes, and offer critiques of students' efforts, everyone benefits. This contact with the real world is further enhanced when the faculty encourages students to participate in film festivals or take part in international exchanges. The name of the game is widening your horizons.

There are three other practical benefits of a good documentary specialist department. The first is that you should be able earn a master of fine arts (MFA), which is indispensible for any future teaching job you have in mind. Usually, work for the degree necessitates you making a major documentary, which is wonderful practice and also gives you a major calling card to show future employers. However, many MFA programs don't want students who have just graduated with a BA. They want students who have some life and production experience and can create a diverse resource pool of talent. Also, many MFA programs require GRE test scores, and these tests can be tough if you don't take them seriously.

The second gain, underestimated but of major importance, is that while studying in a specialist department, you have the ability to build a community of colleagues who can help you after graduation. This community of friends can be an immense help. While preparing this book, I looked at a recent alumni newsletter of my old film department at Stanford University. What surprised and delighted me was the number of references to producers bringing in their old friends as camerapeople, directors suggesting their old buddies as writers on a new project, or both putting work and contacts in the direction of their old roommates.

The final plus of a good film program is that you should be able to emerge on graduation with two or three good examples of your work to show to future employers. In fact, if you can't do that, you will be at a distinct disadvantage in finding a job. The reason is simple. Employers (except if new grads are going for teaching posts) will only be mildly interested in the diploma and the list of courses you have taken. What they do want to see is a demonstration of your real film skills, as writer, cameraperson, or editor. Hence, it is absolutely vital that you emerge with a few films under your arms or a good demonstration reel that exhibits your best talents.

Film-department Drawbacks

Unfortunately, the film-department system also has many drawbacks, the key one being inexperienced faculty. Often, film theoreticians and scholars are given practical courses to teach and then only learn the material and equipment five minutes before class. This is allied to the problem of employing instructors who have studied everything from books (and have possibly even written them) but have never made a film in their lives. This problem occurs particularly frequently in directing and writing classes. So beware.

The ideal is the instructor who has a vast experience in filmmaking but who also knows how to teach. The only problem here is the excellent instructor who is, however, totally devoted to only one school of film-making, usually cinema verité. This was the case at the National Film and Television School in Britain, where cinema verité (or observational cinema) was the one and only accepted gospel for years. Although an excellent technique, cinema verité is only one among many, and I believe students should be allowed to try everything.

After dealing with experts, we come to expenses. The hungry, penniless art student is of course a cliché, but it is now being transferred to the film student. While state schools may charge low fees, university courses at some schools, such as Stanford or New York University, can cost the student upwards of $30,000 a year. Over two or three years, student debt can amount to over $90,000. When I was researching this book a film-maker friend of mine, Minda Martin, wrote me the following:

> I told my brothers who complain about my student loan debt that I bought an education while they bought a home. My student loan debt is a great burden. While my education offered me the illusion of upward-class mobility in that I teach at a university and make $50K, the loan payments have kept me in the same economic status as the graduate student living hand to mouth.

So a question, unanswerable but vital to think about is, "Is the film department worth the money?"

Though one can criticize much of the curriculum of the average film department (if such an institution exists), one overall criticism applies to most of them. This is the failure of the film program to teach a few basic professional courses that could vitally help students after graduation. Here I'm referring to courses related to film budgeting, contracts, serious proposal writing, distribution, and professional documentary producing.

To a certain extent, I understand that failure. When I studied law at the university, I did two courses on Roman law (very vital, of course, in the twentieth and twenty-first centuries) but had nothing on tax law. The attitude was, "We are academics, not grubby money seekers, and you'll acquire your professional skills later." Over the years, things have changed, and I'm told today lawyers learn everything about derivatives, income-tax avoidance, and second-tier mortgages. If a fusty profession like law can accommodate to the reality of today's world, then so can film programs.

My last complaint about film departments is their increasing tendency to separate themselves from television training. This is a mistake. These days as a director, writer, cameraperson, or editor, one often flits between film and TV work. What you learn for one medium is so easy to apply to the other. So if you do head for film school, see whether it also includes television studies, which can add an extra string to your bow.

The Crucial Questions

Balancing the pros and cons of attending a film department is not easy. The crucial questions to ask are what are your personal needs, and does a selected film program answer them at an affordable cost in time and money? While not a wild enthusiast for film schools, I think the best of them can provide a tremendous push to the keen and ambitious student.

While my personal experience of film departments and professional schools is obviously limited, I would like to mention three or four I've seen that I would thoroughly recommend to any student. Although all specialize in documentary, their fees vary enormously. In no particular order, the schools include Stanford University, the University of North Texas at Denton, Columbia College Chicago, City of Westminster College in London, and Ireland's National Film School, Institute of Art, Design, and Technology, in Dun Laoghaire, near Dublin.

When I ask myself why these particular schools lodge in my mind, the answer is very clear. All boast outstanding film instructors who are or have been very successful film professionals, who know how to teach and inspire, and who are devoted to their students.

At Columbia College Chicago, the film department was led for years by Michael Rabiger, a brilliant Englishman, whose books and teaching methods have shown the torch to endless students. Since his retirement, Australian Russell Porter has continued the tradition of excellence. Similar things can be said about Ben Levin and Melinda Levin in North Texas, Jan Krawitz and Kris Samuelson at Stanford, Joost Hunningher in London, and Donald Taylor Black in Dublin.

In short, the inspired instructor is the key . . . but therein lies the rub. You hear of someone's reputation, because of him or her you join the department, and the person promptly retires. So you have to be a little bit careful. Usually, if the department has a high reputation sustained over many years, then you know you're OK.

In practice, you'll find that the good instructor usually rises above the role of teacher to become coach, life guide, and friend. I had two instructors like that, Henry Breitrose and George Stoney. Put simply, they showed me the way, encouraged me by example, and from then on, I've never looked back. If you find someone like that at college, and these instructors exist everywhere, then you'll be very lucky.

3. First Steps in the Real World

YOU'RE BETWEEN THE AGES OF twenty and twenty-six. Possibly, you've just finished film school. Or maybe you're older, and you've learned a little bit about film somewhere and want to take the whole business of documentary more seriously. You feel a little bit lost, a little bit in limbo. Over numerous black coffees and cappuccinos in small cafés, you wonder how to get ahead and move into the real world of professional filmmaking. This chapter and the next are designed to help you answer those questions.

Increasing Your Professionalism

Until now, in film school or via acquaintances or associates, you've acquired a certain knowledge about documentary filmmaking. You've made a few short films (that your friends and colleagues have praised to the skies), and you know your way a little bit around film and video equipment. What you now have to ask yourself is what is the serious level of your professionalism? Your probable answer is "not very much," and as you swallow another cup of overpriced Starbucks or Seattle's Best Coffee brew of the day, you acknowledge that the first thing you have to do is supplement both your technical and commercial skills.

How can you do this? Very easily, by taking advantage of short-term film and video courses that are now given almost everywhere in the United States and England, for relatively low fees. How do you find such courses? By using the Internet and simply Googling "documentary film workshops" and your local area. Do that, and you'll probably be amazed at what's offered and the number of workshops available.

Most of them are there to make money. Many hype their courses to the sky and promise that you can become the new Michael Moore in a day, a week, a month at the most. So you have to be careful. Take your time looking around. Ask your friends or former participants how good the courses are, what they learned, and what was helpful. This way you should be able to sort the good from the bad.

The courses normally split into those giving advanced technical training and those devoted to helping you develop your ongoing projects. While it's beyond the scope and ability of this book to list all the courses available, I thought I'd mention a few that have caught my eye over the years and that are worth investigating. They include:

- San Francisco Film Society. The organization offers courses in advanced editing, shooting digital documentaries, publicity and marketing, grant applications, and many others.
- Manhattan Edit Workshop. Besides courses in editing and filmmaking workshops, the center also offers equipment access and screenings.
- Community Film Workshop of Chicago. The concentration is on learning advanced video editing.
- Kansas Annual Documentary Workshop.
- Rockport Workshops, Maine.
- New Mexico Documentary Workshop. The courses are specially geared to help Native American and Hispanic filmmakers.
- Met Film School, London. This institution offers three- and four-week courses in advanced documentary filming.

If you want to go wider and look at documentary from a broader commercial perspective, then the following centers may be useful.

- Sundance Institute Documentary Film Program. Editing skills are taught alongside story development.
- Realscreen Summit. Annual workshops, sponsored by *Realscreen Magazine*, include courses on running your own production company, alternative funding, and perfecting pitching skills.
- International Documentary Association. This organization, based in Los Angeles, offers a variety of workshops, usually in conjunction with its annual film festival.

- Discovery Campus. Besides again emphasizing the teaching of pitching skills, the Discovery Campus (based in Munich, Germany) aims very hard at teaching commercial survival skills. Thus, one of its more interesting courses lists itself as "Seriously on Series: The Art and Business of Making Documentary TV Series."
- Greenhouse Film Centre. Greenhouse is a revolving documentary training program working out of Israel, Turkey, and Holland. Using European Union funds, it is aimed at teaching development skills from proposal through the pitch to the actualizing of production.

Self-assessment and Focusing Your Aims

Over time and multiple course attendances, your money runs out, but your skills improve. You learn to edit like Sergei Eisenstein and to film better than Haskell Wechsler. And though you haven't yet sold your thirteen- part TV series on "Looking for Love in the Twenty-first Century," you're pretty sure you know how to do so, if only you can get down to writing the proposal. It is at this point, or maybe even before, that you need to sit back and begin to ponder some deeper questions. These are soul-searching questions that have nothing to do with film equipment but everything to do with your filmic future. You have climbed the mountain. The world-renowned guru, Abasingh (formerly Joe Klein), sits in his cave surrounded by the most beautiful acolytes. Abasingh, a former employee of Paramount, who has found nirvana, asks you, "OK, my worthy friend and seeker after truth. What career do you want? And how important is money?" You probably can't answer the questions, at least not all in one go, but as you slide down the snow-capped slopes, the guru's questions keep repeating. "Who am I? What are my objectives? And what do I really think about financial survival?"

In the past, you may have thought of yourself under the generic term *filmmaker*. It could be that as you start your real professional career, that is not enough. Maybe now is the time for you to think what you really want to do, what role suits you best, and where you want to put your efforts. Earlier, you thought of yourself as a future Spielberg, but now, after self-examination, you realize you are more interested in editing than directing. A year ago, your life was dominated by cameras and lenses, but now you see that writing interests you more. Or, strangest of all, you feel yourself attracted by the role of producer. The choice doesn't matter, and maybe in the end as a filmmaker, you'll combine many roles. However,

I suggest that in the beginning, it's helpful to focus your energy in one direction and put all your effort into getting there.

Besides this exercise in trying to understand where your potential lies and what film task makes you most happy, you have to ask yourself, "What films do I want to make?" Up to now, the question hasn't come up. You've dutifully shot class films and by chance found an interesting subject for your thesis film. Or, as a self-taught filmmaker, maybe you've started off with a film about your family. But all these are one-offs, and now some serious time has to be devoted to deciding what kind of films you want to make.

Do you want to make popular commercial film series like *Boys' Toys* or passionate political films like *Bowling for Columbine*? Do you want to make small, personal, quirky, funny films like Alan Berliner's *Wide Awake*, or do you want to go for the impersonal best seller? Does biography fascinate you, or do you feel yourself drawn to the investigatory social film?

Now realistically, in the beginning of your career, you'll probably be up for anything that comes your way. You just want to make a living and get a toe in the industry door. And maybe you'll continue that way. But if you do have a craving for a particular kind of film or an abhorrence for a particular genre, best to acknowledge it early. You'll be happier that way.

Some years ago, I made a lot of films about hospitals. It took me four years to realize I hated the inside of hospitals and didn't want to touch the subject again. I also realized fairly early on I wasn't cut out to make films on searing social issues. Gradually, I realized my penchant was for making films on historical or music subjects, and I've been content ever since.

The final self-awareness question you have to grapple with is, "How important is money for me?" Are you content with the small, rented, one-bedroom apartment? Do you aspire to the house in the suburbs? Do you want a swanky car, or will a beaten-up, old Volkswagen be fine for you? Is the ability to save a little each month important, or do you say to yourself, "Let the future take care of itself"?

Well, you know you're probably not going to become a millionaire making documentaries, but it's also clear certain kinds of documentary work make more money than others. For example, if you work as a regular on a specific series for PBS, the odds are you'll have more to take home at the end of the month than the average independent filmmaker. Those are the blunt facts of life. But then you have to ask whether churning out, say, animal films or essays on religious ethics week after week is what you really want.

Let me give you an example from life. A few months ago, my distributor, a lovely Canadian, phoned me with tears in his voice. No, I made that up the bit about "tears," but he did phone me. Basically, he was asking me to abandon my one-off films that took me a year and a half to make and instead to start doing a series on crime and prisons. Why, because that's where the money was and what the market wanted. Sadly, because I really wouldn't have minded making some money, I told him that wasn't for me.

Problems arise when your goals become confused. I have a friend Dina, who makes very personal documentaries, mainly about her family, her friends, poets, and political struggles that interest her. Her films are passionate, usually very good, but get shown to limited audiences. Of necessity, the financial returns on her films are very small, yet she longs for the Broadway lights and an improved bank balance. I tell her, very gently, that with the kind of films she makes she is unlikely to realize these dreams. Most of the time she refuses to hear me and becomes distressed at her situation. Had she really seen how her goals clash and had acted accordingly, I think she would be a much happier person.

What is the underlying message? Know yourself. Assess your potential, and define your objectives. Do all that, and life becomes fairly simple, and you can spend your time making great films with a clear mind. You know what you want, you know where you want to go, you know your abilities . . . so there is no reason why you shouldn't achieve all your objectives.

4. Vital Survival Knowledge

FILM SCHOOL TENDS TO BE a delightful period. You glide through three or four years having fun, occasionally bitching at teachers or assignments but on the whole enjoying yourself. That's fine, but it can also be too much of a passive experience. Equipment was automatically supplied from the film cage in the hall. You just signed up and took what was available. Exercises were rigidly formulated, and for the most part you turned them in on time. And never ever did you have to consider, "How does all this help me make a living?" But now the sign says, "Get with it," indicating you have to make a drastic change from passive to active mode. This means, for starters, mastering both equipment and technical changes and at another level becoming market savvy.

Mastering Equipment and Technical Changes

Until the late seventies, most documentaries were made on 16 mm film, using simple flat-bed editing tables like the Moviola or Steenbeck. You bought or hired your Arriflex, Bolex, or Beaulieu camera, and that was that. You could have fallen asleep like Rip Van Winkle, woken after five years, seen little change in the film equipment, and continued exactly where you left off.

Today, with the revolutionary switch to video, change is the name of the game, tapeless cameras, P2 cards, and new work-flow patterns. Once, you just bought a camera. Now, after going through an alphabetical and numerical maze of camera markings such as DVX, XYZ, ABC, PD100, PD170, and the like, you have to decide whether you want an optical stabilizer, flash memory, hard drive, HD potential, progressive recording, or gen lock. I am surprised manufacturers don't tell us that the cameras also make toast. No wonder camera courses now last a lifetime instead of two days. But that's not the end. Next time, you will find even more changes and almost have to go back to square one.

Similar changes are affecting all editing systems and sound recording. You thought you were happy with your Avid Xpress system or Final Cut Pro programs. Well, think again. A new program has just come out enhancing your ability to create fantastic titling and superb rainbow credits, and everyone is getting on the bandwagon. So those old programs have to be junked unless you want to be regarded as an industrial primitive.

OK, I know I am overstressing the situation, but the bottom line is you had better make yourself familiar with the changes, or you'll be very hampered professionally. This situation can also be seen in the effects game.

Once, effects in documentaries were mostly limited to fades and dissolves. Documentary had to be seen to be real, and tampering with the image was just not done. Today, all those rules and maxims are up for debate. Documentary style has broken through all sorts of barriers, and the use of effects is commonplace, particularly in history documentaries such as Simcha Jacobovici's *Exodus Decoded*. This means that you must familiarize yourself with techniques such as the use of computer-generated images (CGIs). The easiest way to do that is by going to an effects house, telling them you are thinking of using some effects in your next film, and asking if they can put on a demonstration for you. Most houses will be more than willing to show you what they can offer. The drawback, of course, is that CGIs cost the earth. Recently, some houses have come down in price, so there may be hope. However, don't be too dismayed, as most editing-software programs now include a wide array of animation and motion effects, as well as extensive graphics programs.

The Need to Know the Market

In the past, the sheer joy of filmmaking was an end in itself. You'd made a film, shown it to your friends, and risen in their estimation. Now you want to do more. You want to make films that sell and that will provide you with an income. To do that, to realize that goal, you must familiarize yourself with the marketplace and be prepared if necessary to accommodate yourself to it (see chapter 12, "Making Money," for more on this topic). This means knowing what is out there—knowing the structure of the markets, what is being made, for whom, and what the broadcasters seem to want. Let's start with the television-market structure.

In practice, the market is split into what might loosely be called the first market and second market. The first market includes the principal public and private networks in each country. In the United States, that means the commercial networks, PBS, and cable channels, such as A&E, HBO, Discovery, and CourtTV. In the United Kingdom, we are talking about the BBC, Channel 4, and BSkyB, while in Germany, we are referring to ZDF, Spiegel, and ARD. In France, the main players are CanalPlus, ARTE, FR2, and FR3. The second market includes players like Globo Sat in Brazil, Rai-Sat and CNI in Italy, Bravo and HBO in Latin America, and CanalPlus in northern Europe.

On the surface, all this looks great. In practice, competition among filmmakers to get their films on has created a buyers' market. This means fees for the first market, which is your major consideration, have been severely reduced.

The final point about marketing is that because of the Internet and the ability to make DVDs at a low cost, new delivery systems may well be taking hold. This is so important that I've left the subject for a discussion in depth in chapter 12.

What films are stations buying? To know that, you have to keep up with the latest trends and see what's popular. You don't necessarily have to emulate the trends, but you must know what's going on. For example, take a moment to look at *TV Guide* or your local newspaper and see what documentaries are being shown. For fun, I did just that, looking at the offerings on National Geographic, A&E, HBO, my local PBS channel, and the History Channel—all of them prime screeners of documentaries. This is a sample of what I found:

Valley of the Wolves
Lost Evidence: Break Out from Normandy
Digging the Bible: Buried Secrets
Alternative Medicine: Acupuncture
The Brain Story: All in the Mind (series)
Santos Dumont: The Father of Aviation
Jerusalem–Berlin and Back
Elephant Diaries, a series about elephant calves
Aircraft Carrier
This World: India's Missing Girls
Sadhus of India
Franklin Delano Roosevelt

The list is salutary for one thing. It shows what the networks think the public wants to watch, and very few of them are social documentaries.

It is also worthwhile trying to see what's happening with documentary series. Are there popular, ongoing ones to which you could contribute? Does a particular series trigger any ideas in your mind? As I said before, my distributor wanted me to create a series about crime and punishment. It wasn't my forte, but I knew he was absolutely right in assessing what the public might want to see. He was also right to stress the word *series* because often these are more saleable than one-off documentaries. They fill up programming time nicely and with luck draw captive audiences week after week.

Besides thinking what to make for the market, you should also be thinking about changes in filmic methods. Before, you would have done a straight documentary. Maybe now you want to do a drama doc, as the form is becoming more and more popular. It is also worthwhile to observe stylistic changes in documentary. I've already mentioned the increasing use of CGIs. Alongside this, one can also mention the use of reconstructions, drama elements, and animation in major documentaries. *Waltz with Bashir* was done entirely as animation. A documentary I saw a month ago about business moguls used a mock Monopoly board on which model figures advanced and retreated as they drowned in money. Altogether, it was a very humorous illustration of the machinations of the moguls. So it seems anything goes, with the only criteria being whether the effect works and improves the documentary.

Information Sources

In the few paragraphs above, I stressed the necessity of keeping up with current developments in the documentary film world. How do you do this? Although you can attend forums and screenings, most of your information is going to come from newspapers, magazines, and the Internet. However, now there's going to be a subtle change in your reading. Previously, you probably studied documentary through the prisms of art or culture. For "Film Theory 201" and "Documentary History 322," you were directed to magazines such as *Screen*, *Sight and Sound*, *Jump Cut*, and *Film Quarterly*. If you were really keen and wanted to show off, you also picked up *The Velvet Light Trap* or *Cahiers du Cinema*. Via your studies, you learned to use exalted terms such as *female gaze*, *iconic*, *indexal*, and *scopophilia* and absorbed all the latest theoretical articles by Michael Renov, Brian Winston, and Bill Nichol—all good reading for a dark, snowy night in the wilds of Montana.

All that has to change. Now you have to shift your gaze to much more down-to-earth and prosaic reading that will inform you directly about equipment change and marketing trends. You have to shift from left brain to right brain, or is it vice versa? It doesn't really matter, because it's clear your reading habits will have to be revised. Again, without making exhaustive lists, I suggest the following magazines and newspapers to help keep up with the latest trends in the market.

For information about equipment, I'd use

HDVideo Pro
DV
HDTV Magazine
American Photographer

I'd also spend some time scanning the catalogues of big equipment houses, such as B and H.

In regard to public relations, the film industry, and general broadcasting, try

Government Video
Event DV magazine
Broadcasting and Cable
Broadcast magazine
TVB Television Broadcasting
Hollywood Reporter
Variety

The two documentary magazines most concerned with marketing and documentary issues are *Realscreen* (check the Web site), which is published in Toronto, and *International Documentary* (check the Web site), which originates in Los Angeles. With *Realscreen*, the emphasis is on the world of cable. It also publishes *International Broadcast Guide*, which contains valuable information on broadcasters around the world. The information is very practical and tells about factual strands, themes, and length of favored programs. The guide also gives station biographies, the names of commissioning editors, and their contact information, including e-mail addresses. *International Documentary*, for its part, includes a listing of some of the main upcoming U.S. film festivals and a monthly guide to cable programming. Its most useful section, however, may be its listing of current funding opportunities, telling what's out there and where and when to apply for grants.

A third specialist documentary magazine I consider to be very useful is *DOX*, published in Denmark but available in Britain and the United States. Although *DOX* has become essential documentary reading in Europe, its European bias shouldn't put off Americans. The magazine provides essential information for anyone interested in the European scene. While focusing on production and distribution possibilities, it also publishes some excellent documentary articles, probably slightly more academic than those appearing in *Realscreen* and in the *International Documentary* magazine. It also publishes a useful *European Producers Guide* somewhat similar to that put out by *Realscreen*.

One other interesting piece of writing to look at, more pamphlet than magazine, is *The Documentary Cookbook*, distributed by the Center for New Documentary at the University of California, Berkeley. *The Cookbook*—lovely name—consists of a few pages of very succinct advice on low-budget filmmaking put out by Jon Else and some of the other faculty at Berkeley's Graduate School of Journalism. The advice is very useful and practical but is mainly aimed at the documentary filmmaker who already knows the ropes and is trying to reach a large television audience. The simplest way to find and read the pamphlet is just to Google "Berkeley documentary cookbook."

Besides the occasional browsing of the above magazines, it is also useful to keep your eyes open for articles on documentary in newspapers such as the *New York Times, Los Angeles Times*, and *Wall Street Journal*. The articles (at least in the first two) tend to be few and far between, but when they do appear, they usually offer a mine of information on some new aspect of documentary practice and marketing.

Finally, I suggest that it is essential to look at *TV Guide*. The magazine is a weekly and not everyone's cup of tea. For instance, you may not be interested in celebrity interviews and gossip, nor may you want to do crossword puzzles or read your horoscope. On the other hand, it is an invaluable tool if you want to see what documentaries are being screened every day on television and where broadcasters are putting their money.

5. Working for Others

DECISION TIME HAS COME. Take off for Europe? Go into your father's furniture business? Try to get into a Wall Street firm? No, maybe not after the last crisis. Or continue with film? Finally, you decide to bite the bullet and devote yourself to professional documentary filmmaking. In practice, this means you have three options before you:

- Teaching
- Working for others
- Making your own films

The first option, teaching, probably includes the possibility of your continuing filmmaking, which is fine. The second choice may offer you a full career or more often may be the path that ultimately leads you to go independent. This chapter deals with the first two career possibilities.

Teaching

Almost every major city boasts of a film department. If a town doesn't have a film program, it's just not hip, not with it. And even in those universities that believe themselves to be above the fray, film or TV studies normally creeps into communications or English departments. All of which means there is a fair demand for film academics.

Once, you could find an academic film job if you roughly knew one end of a camera from the other. Times have changed. Today, most serious academic institutions will demand a terminal degree from those applying for a full-time job. This means a PhD if you intend to teach the more academic film studies and an MFA if you are going to teach practical courses. If looking for employment as a part-time adjunct documentary teacher, then you can sometime get away without possessing the MFA. The problem with adjunct teaching is that it's demanding, is badly paid, and usually offers few welfare benefits, if any. However, it may be a tad better than waiting on tables and keeps you in touch with the profession.

You can, of course, look for a teaching job immediately after getting a degree, but I'd wait a bit. Most places will want to see that you have made a few films and have gotten a little bit of experience before employing you. So time usually increases your chances.

Schools and departments vary, so it's wise to examine very carefully what's being offered before accepting the job. Find out what courses you'll be expected to teach. Are you really qualified to teach them, or will you be able to teach them after a little bit of homework? Equally important, does the department encourage its faculty to make films? Will it allow you to use its equipment and facilities when you want to make your own films, and does it allow you time off or a sabbatical to get back to film-making? These are important questions because unless they are answered positively, you may find yourself getting farther and farther away from filmmaking. If the department does support faculty filmmaking, then you've probably come to a good place and can join the ranks of the best of the teachers, those who teach from practice and experience.

In terms of getting to know the academic market, it might be worth your while joining the University Film and Video Association (UFVA). This is basically an American umbrella organization linking most people interested in teaching film and television. The UFVA holds an annual conference in August that besides offering screenings, discussions, wine, and a lot of fun also provides an opportunity to meet academics, talk to them, and find out informally what's going on in the teaching world. The UFVA also publishes a bulletin that often advertises the latest film-teaching jobs. Another worthwhile organization to join is the Broadcast Education Association (BEA). Both the BEA and UFVA support documentary groups for their members.

Working for Others

If you decide to start your film career by looking for a full- or part-time job, you first have to think about what jobs are out there and how to locate them. Second, you have to consider how best to get your foot in the door. Lastly, once you've got the job, you have to consider how to maximize all the opportunities it offers you.

Job Opportunities

In looking for a job, you may want to cast your net very wide and start thinking outside the usual parameters. It helps to take a moment to quantify your talents. What can you do? What are you capable of? How would you describe yourself? You are certainly not just a filmmaker. You are a person who can handle a camera, edit, tell a story, write, organize, and deal well with people. You are used to facing deadlines, dealing with sudden problems, meeting people, and confronting strangers and are skilled in the art of persuasion. So what organizations do you know in any way related to film and film activities that might be able use your many gifts?

Well, obviously first on your list are any local TV stations and any local production companies. Those are clearly the first places to start. But what about advertising offices? Couldn't they use skills just like yours? They need people who can write well, can visualize stories, can think fast, and know something about film. Doesn't that describe you?

Then, public and private corporations, hospitals, colleges, and the like could well use your talents. These are areas definitely not to be ignored. Until recently, many of these places contracted out their training films and their public-relations films. Now, more and more of these institutions are finding it cheaper and more efficient to do the work themselves. Since the spread of low-cost video, they have started installing their own in-house film-and-video departments. If you get involved, you may find yourself making a tremendous number of films very fast under comparatively little supervision. You have a wonderful opportunity to train, learn, and develop very fast.

Last but not least are the burgeoning high-tech companies. Here, too, many have installed small filmmaking departments to cater to their internal needs. Many of them, however, are also interested in your wider skills. This I particularly noted when looking at the postgraduation histories of alumni of Stanford's documentary department. Stanford is situated in Palo Alto, the very heart of Silicon Valley, Hewlett-Packard, and Bill Gates country. Taking advantage of that fact, it seems many Stanford MFA graduates applied to local high-tech industries and were taken on as much for their all-round skills as for their filmmaking abilities.

Locating Job Possibilities

Once you know the job areas that interest you, you have to get down to business. That means hunting down addresses, telephone numbers, and e-mail addresses, and making contacts. Some of this information you'll already have via friends, acquaintances, and teachers. Yet, that information is very sporadic. You have to get serious and thorough and start making concrete main lists of everyone you want to contact. OK, OK! I know that sounds overwhelming, and already your brain feels tired and overburdened, although you haven't even begun looking or listing. Now the good news. You can relax because most of that work has already been done for you, with the answers to be found in various easily accessible professional guides.

Let's just begin with the addresses of TV stations and identification of personnel. They can be found in various PBS directories, which you can locate online and in the Realscreen and EDN (European Documentary Network) guides, already mentioned. Most of these guides give address, name of department head, telephone number, and e-mail.

If you want to work for a production company, the best starting point is to turn to the film and TV production directories put out by most cities. Go to the Web for the international compendium of film and TV production entities at productionhub.com's site; a search under "production directory and guide for broadcasting, TV, film, and video" should bring up a Web page that has a list of locations internationally. New York, for example, puts out the yearly *Production Directory and Guide for Broadcasting, TV, Film, and Video.* This guide lists production houses, animation houses, special-effects centers, television studios, and the like. In other words, you can find the addresses of every single film or TV production branch in your immediate area that interests you. Similarly, you might want to turn to Mandy's *International Film and TV Production Resources,* which lists very similar information, as well as jobs available in production crews and new media. These kinds of guides are not limited to major urban areas but are available in most large cities and states. Thus, while researching this chapter, I turned up production guides for Illinois and Oklahoma and would have found more had I not felt the desperate need for a cup of coffee.

Like film, advertising and public-relations firms have their own cocooned world, habits, and styles. While most of the big advertising and PR offices work out of New York, Chicago, Los Angeles, and San Francisco, there probably are quite a few local advertising offices close to you, where jobs might even be more accessible than in the big cities. Two names worthwhile noting are Manpower Inc., the largest employer in the world of part-time and full-time people, and Craigslist, which lists state and city jobs in radio, TV, and film. Although the Yellow Pages may provide a few addresses for PR and advertising companies, you should also become familiar with the main advertising magazines and see whom you can locate from their pages. The main trade magazines are

- *Advertising Age*
- *Adweek*
- *Brand Republic*
- *Commercial Art*

It is also advisable to read the magazines so that you can familiarize yourself with the area but more on that later.

Locating high-tech jobs and vacancies in hospital, municipal, or college departments is a little more haphazard. Here a visit to your local library or municipal offices may well pay off in giving you leads, addresses, and information as to what exists and who are the main players in each area.

Getting Your Feet in the Door

Having identified your targets, learn all you can about your possible employer. You must do some preliminary homework. What is the company history? What exactly does it do? What areas does it specialize in? Where possible, speak to people familiar with the company or people who've worked for it or done business with it. The idea is to come to the interview (when and if granted) well prepared. If applying to a company that makes medical videos, try to learn as much as you can about the field or at least do a little preparation. If you are turning to a high-tech company, what do they make? And who are their competitors? If applying to an advertising company, find out what companies it represents. Have you seen any of their ads (and the answer must be "yes"), and what do you think of them?

Maybe I'm asking for the impossible here. How can you possibly find out who the competitors of a high-tech firm are or why films can help in advertising a medical product? Most times, that information will be beyond your grasp. That's OK so long as you grasp the main point—that when applying for a job, you get as much information as you can about your potential boss. That information also helps you in writing and toning your curriculum vitae (CV) or résumé, which you'll have to submit before any interview.

The good CV or résumé is the key that unlocks at least the first door, and it should be sent by mail, not e-mail, as that easily gets overlooked. The document should be short, relevant, and probably not over two pages . . . as most filmmakers' reading span is extremely limited. Start in the present, and go back. Don't bother to go into school grades or college grades or list individual courses, but do highlight or emphasize anything that proves your excellence.

What you need to stress is anything that makes you stand out from the mob. Your prospective employer probably won't be interested in hearing that like Ingmar Bergman, you started projecting films in your nursery at the age of three. But he or she will be interested in hearing that you won your local area documentary competition three times in a row or that you've had two articles printed in the *New Yorker*.

You also gear your CV or résumé to the nature of the job you are looking for. So, yes, you spent a semester interning at Hewlett-Packard or acted as a volunteer orderly in your local veterans' hospital. Even better if you've already interned on a few documentaries.

What you'll discover, sadly and regretfully, is that most of the time your prospective boss will not be interested in your degrees (unless you are a Yale or Harvard graduate) and that your hard-earned BA in English literature counts for naught. Even harder to stomach is the fact that they'll only take a cursory glance at your diploma in film studies from your local college. Instead what they'll be looking for is proof you know something about filmmaking and know how to shoot, edit, or write. If you can show them a reel of your work or examples of films you've edited or scripts you've written, then they'll be delighted. And any previous work experience will be a plus.

Together with your CV or résumé, send a cover letter. That will set out why you want the job, maybe give a broader picture of your personality, again express how good you are, and say why working with this particular firm is tailor-made for you. All right, so you exaggerate a bit, but that's the nature of the game. You have to distinguish yourself from all the other applicants and prove you have fire in the belly.

I used to run a production office in Manhattan, and we probably got about five letters a week from job applicants, just writing in hopeful and out-of-the-blue. I used to look them over, searching for something different—a spark, an imaginative approach, something unique they had done, some original thinking, evidence of a sense of humor—and then file them away. When I had time, I wrote a short letter of thanks for contacting me. Most of the time, as we were only a small office, we had nothing going and couldn't be of any help to the applicants. Occasionally, however, the letter came in just as we were starting a new film, and I wrote, "Come, let's talk to you." I also went back to my files and invited a few of the applicants whose letters I had starred to come in for a discussion. Over the years, I think we employed about five assistants that way, two of whom became permanent staff.

The moral of the above is that timing can be very important. And you may not and most likely cannot know what is going on at any firm that would allow you to work that timing. But after months of idleness comes a rush of work, and then suddenly people are needed, and jobs are open. It's very much a matter of luck. One other point I'd stress is to drop reminders, a note, a telephone call, an e-mail. They can be very simple. "Dear Mr. Smith, I talked to you about a month ago. You said you had no work, but that some might be in the offing and that I should stay in touch. I wonder if there has been any change in the situation. Yours sincerely, etc., etc."

Getting a good job can be a matter of luck but it is also a matter of passion and determination. The Oscar-winning director Mark John Harris started off as a newspaper reporter who wanted to make films. Along the way, Mark went to New York to meet with producer Richard de Rochemont (*March of Time*). De Rochemont asked Mark two questions: "Is your father rich?" and "Have you written a best-selling novel yet? Those are the two best ways I know to get into film." Undaunted, Mark wrote to Stimson Bullitt, a man whom he'd met at a job interview. Bullitt owned three television stations and was interested in making documentary films for his station. As Mark puts it,

> I wrote him an impassioned letter telling him how much I wanted to make documentaries. Whether it was the letter, or my year and a half experience as a reporter, this time I impressed him. He telephoned a few weeks later and invited me for an interview. A month later I was working for the documentary department of KGW-TV.

Cameraman/director Mark Benjamin's story is another example of determination bringing employment. Mark was a photographer and had worked for months on a color story for *Life* magazine. Suddenly, *Life* closed up shop, and his story was killed. Then, Mark met a documentary-film crew in Jerusalem and became their assistant.

I forced myself on them. I was so depressed. They met me, they liked me. They knew what had happened, that I had been out on my first *Life* assignment and the magazine closed. So they took pity on me, and then they made me their assistant cameraman. That turned out to be a defining moment in my life.

Exploiting Opportunities, or Mr. Keen Comes to Town

To your surprise and delight, you get a job. You arrive on time (in fact, you learn to arrive early and leave late to show you're keen). You get introduced to staff, get shown around, and then . . . you wait. The odds are that in the beginning you'll be given all the menial jobs. You'll run errands, make the coffee, answer the phone, and do the copying and the filing. And you'll begin to wonder, "Where does filmmaking come into all this?" Gradually, however. things will change, probably starting in the editing room. Here your job may be keeping records or digitizing material. Occasionally, you'll also be asked to go out on a shoot, mainly acting as tea boy or girl and assistant cameraperson.

The weeks go by. You begin to see how things are done, and your boss begins to see that you're quite reliable. Then the responsibilities grow. You handle bills. You start to fix appointments. You handle all the film and video logs, and you begin to shoot and edit small sequences. Your boss may also try you out on writing a small PR film.

As time passes by and you get to be comfortable, what else should you be doing? You should be learning the total business, not just your job, and you should be learning new skills. For example, you should be observing how your boss deals with clients and looks for new work. You should try and participate in his discussions as to the pros and cons of buying new equipment. You ask the main cameraperson to instruct you on the various cameras held in the store, and you don't blush to ask the editor to demonstrate new programs to you. And you observe the small things. You take note of the way the certificates and festival awards are displayed to catch the attention of the clients. You always remember to get fresh pastries and bagels when clients are due to come in. And you note when to joke and when to be formal.

So you go on, day by day, week by week, all the time learning a little bit more of the business and taking a little bit more responsibility. You can continue like this forever, but how do you advance up the ladder? By becoming proactive. You don't just do your job, but you start thinking ahead. You start to think how you can be of real assistance to your boss, instead of just a useful hired hand. You begin to think how the business can be carried out more efficiently, how it can blossom and expand into new areas. All this can lead to two things. At best, your boss indicates you can become a serious player in the firm. Alternatively, your boss can say, "You're good, but we don't have enough room here, and it's best you move on." If he says that, then it may, in fact, be a blessing because it probably indicates that the time has come for you to go solo. And then comes the real challenge!

6. Becoming an Independent Filmmaker

AN OXYMORON IS A LINKING of two contradictory terms. I was brought up on them and loved them. My favorites were *military intelligence, original copies,* and *open secret.* With time, I added another one, *independent filmmaker.* This term, particularly as applied to documentary, has always seemed to me a joke. As filmmakers we always have our hand out. We beg for money, for support, and without it we're dead or at least pretty sick. Are we independent? No way!

I mention this problem of economic fragility because the word *risk* is the first thing you have to remember when you go out on your own. As an independent, you have to be prepared for risk. Risk is the name of the game. Its second name is uncertainty. These are the basic facts you have to absorb. Yet, as I mentioned in my introduction, other words describe your mad pursuit, such as *fun, worthwhile,* and even, occasionally *financially rewarding.*

If you are making documentary films on an amateur basis, then the above should not worry you or really concern you. You make films as and when you have money, on low budgets, and within your capacities. That's fine, and, occasionally, you'll make a great film. But if you want to become an independent *professional* filmmaker, you have to organize yourself very differently and put yourself into a very different mindset. Becoming an independent documentary filmmaker is simple, at least in theory.

You set up an office, and you go looking for work. What could be easier? Well, a lot of things. For example, you have to start confronting small things like finding ideas, selling them, budgeting for survival, and paying the rent. In the previous chapter, I discussed working for others. If you've done that, you're ahead of the game—you know realistically what life and office organization are all about. Yet, it could be that the majority of us plunge straight in. We know how to make documentaries, or so we think, so let's go out and do it. This chapter is meant to help both of you begin on your own: the filmmaker with a few months' office experience and the intrepid novice with little professional experience but who has the courage to jump in and try the waters.

Setting Up Office

Timing

The decision to set up an office is not easy. You can do that straight from film school, or after trying a number of other jobs, you can decide enough waiting, let's do it. I would suggest, however, there is a definite best moment to make the move. That's when you already have one or two films finished or have just gotten a reasonably large film commission.

The reason for choosing that moment is that the films will give you the financial base to survive the first crucial six months or year. Without some work in hand or a very strong possibility of work coming your way, opening an office is just throwing your money away. In those circumstances, it is much better to work from home, build a small reputation, and only then take the bold move to an office.

Again, be realistic. If you are the filmmaker who is content to work alone and do maybe one film every two years, you don't need an office. You open an office when you are beginning to make a reputation, when films are beginning to come fairly regularly, and when expansion demands it.

Do You Need to Set Up a Company?

As a filmmaker, you can work alone, you can set up a partnership structure, or you can set up a company. The reasons you choose one path above another involve convenience and tax matters. As a sole filmmaker or member of a partnership, you will be responsible for all the debts and obligations of your business. A company, however, is a totally separate legal identity from its members or shareholders. In practice, it means the debts of the company are not your personal debts, even though you are the principal shareholder. That can be very important when a film runs out of control or over budget. Another advantage of setting up a company is that expenses are usually easier to handle, and, according to your state, your business may be open to more tax allowances.

Setting up a company, however, costs money. Not a great deal but there are numerous fees involved. Working alone costs you nothing, and setting up a partnership will only cost you some small legal fees for the partnership agreement. In many cases, you can get along even without a formal agreement.

I've worked in all three situations and have found that working via a company is best. Among other advantages is the fact that you are taken slightly more seriously when applying for work. It may all be psychological, but when a client hears from Tom Smith and from World Television Documentaries Inc., who are really one and the same entity, the odds are they'll pay more attention to the latter.

Other pros and cons need to be taken into consideration before you set up a work base, and they are complex. I advise that you have a discussion with an accountant or lawyer and then decide which work base best suits you.

Where Do You Work From?

Should you work from home in the beginning or rent an office? Your work requirements will give you the answer.

I work as producer, director, and writer. For years, I found it convenient merely to work from the spare room in my house, as my main tools were my typewriter (long since abandoned) and my word processor. Using either of these trusty machines (at least the typewriter was trusty), I could bang out proposals in my role as producer and scripts in my role as writer. When I wanted to make a film, I went out and hired crews, editing rooms, and so forth.

In recent years, with the lowering in the cost of equipment, I've gone out (with a partner) and bought two cameras, sound gear, and two editing consoles. In consequence, we've had to rent some modest offices. As we've made more and more films, we've also needed space for our archives and film library.

One advantage of a decent office is that you can create the best situation for meeting prospective clients. Of course, you can invite them home, hoping they don't trip over the cat food, slip on your old carpet, and wait until you take the milk, coffee, and beer from your fridge in the kitchen. Or you can arrange to meet in a café. You can do all that, but it won't leave a good impression. Far better to let them see your office, your trophies (even student awards), sit them down in one of the two Eames chairs you bought cheaply, and discuss future work over an excellent cup of Madruga-blend coffee from the Flying Goat.

If you rent office space, make sure you calculate all expenses correctly. You should budget at the minimum for six months' rent. After that, you add in (if necessary) cleaning services, telephone, and electricity. Also add in any federal or local taxes you may have to pay. Only by doing all this work can you see realistically what your minimum outgoings are going to be. You may also want to add in the expenses of a bookkeeper, whose services will become more and more important, and general office and equipment insurance. You might also note that you should take out liability insurance on all the films you are making. This will cover you against damage to property and people. You can do this separately for each individual film you make or take out overall film insurance on a yearly basis.

Organizing the Office

My film partner, David, likes working in a mess. To find anything on his desk, you have to go through an archaeological dig. When he's at the Avid editing console, cassettes are scattered all over the place, and half-finished cups of coffee nestle gently among half-opened scripts. Being a more organized kind of guy, I see all this and go mad. To my mind, it's such a disturbingly inefficient way of doing things. Why do I tolerate all this? Because David is a genius and can turn the worst film into a piece of art.

You organize your office so that it becomes an efficient, harmonious place to work and presents an inviting welcome to any clients or guests. To do that, and if you have space, it's best to separate your main office from editing rooms and film and library storage space. The latter should be adequately equipped with shelf space and have a strong security lock on the door. I keep my fax, scanner, and copier in the storage room, but their placement is up to you.

Make sure you give yourself enough space in your editing room for the editing computers and screens. The room also needs racks for supplementary editing equipment and cupboards or shelves to hold editing scripts and archive logbooks. Depending on where you are, it may also be advisable to put in air conditioning. You should also check the electric-power supply to the editing room so that you can cope with any power surge.

The look of your main office is up to you, and you can set it up according to your personal taste while remembering you'll probably be welcoming clients there. I like a few pictures around the place or a few posters. My favorites are Buster Keaton and the Marx Brothers, but you may instead want to put up a picture of your mother-in-law for inspiration.

Production Binders

Above, I mentioned logbooks for editing, scripts, and archives, and they are just a few examples of the logbooks you'll need. Once you are in production, one of your main needs is to find information fast. The way to do that is to create one large loose-leaf production binder or, preferably, separate binders for separate subjects. Generally, I create one binder for editing, tape, sound, and archives logging. This I usually leave in the editing room.

I then make a production binder. This contains all my notes about crew, equipment, locations, contacts, questions for interviews, and releases. My third binder is devoted exclusively to the script. Here I enter versions of my proposal, my script and research notes, and different versions of the script. I also put a copy of the evolving script in the editing binder.

Finally, I create what I call my legal binder. Here I keep all my correspondence, the budget, contracts, and all insurance and legal papers. You can, and many people do, make do with one overall binder. I personally find that gets unwieldy, and I prefer to split everything into the four binders.

To Buy or Rent Equipment

Before the advent of cheap video equipment, I used to rent everything. Altogether, I used to budget a day's shooting, including car, gas, equipment, and crew food at about $1,500. If I had ten days' shooting, I could reckon that basic production expenses were about $15,000. I'd have loved to own my own Betacam camera, but that cost over $15,000. Editing machines, whether film or video, were also expensive, so those two I rented, as well as hiring out an editing room.

Then came the video revolution and with it a change in thinking. A good basic minicassette camera, suitable for most work, should not cost more than $6,000. Even the newest noncassette cameras are not that expensive. Editing equipment with a good program should similarly not cost more than $8,000. If you add in a really good tripod (essential for small-camera shooting), some mikes, a mixer, and a small light kit, then you are ready to go, shoot, and edit for about $16,000. All this argues that where possible, you should buy some minimum equipment rather than rent it. You'll recoup the expenses on one film alone.

Occasionally, you'll be confronted by special situations that can't be handled by your equipment—underwater equipment, heavy lighting, specialist cameras, dolly tracks, and the like. In that case, rent. Otherwise, your minimum equipment should be enough to get you going.

I know cameras change and that every year sees a new gizmo. The same is true for editing programs. You can ignore all that. Maybe every three or four years, you might have to buy something new, but on the whole, your basic equipment should keep you going for a long time.

If you do buy equipment, make sure it is insured both while in the office and out on location. Failure to do that will cost you dearly.

Working with Partners

You are the only one who can judge whether you need a partner or not. The decision usually rests on whether you are comfortable working alone and have the skills to work alone or whether you like working as a team and need the stimulus and help of a second or third partner.

On the psychological level, I think having a partner to whom you can confide troubles and with whom you can plot strategies can be immensely helpful. Over coffee, you can toss ideas at each other, examine them, analyze them, see where they lead you.

Your partner suggests a film on new hospital surgical techniques. You are not fond of that but suddenly start thinking about children and hospitals. Gradually, the idea crystallizes between you about a film on children's fears before operations.

Someone comes to you with a film idea. It seems excellent, but in your eyes there are too many technical problems to be overcome. You explain this to your partner, who reassures you as to how the problems can be overcome. If you were working alone, you would probably have struggled endlessly with the problem and then maybe, but just maybe, gone to seek a friend's help.

I think it's also easier for two people to handle financial problems than one. Expenses are split, rent is split, and I think the arrangement—provided there is real sharing—ensures a great financial stability.

The last, but not least, advantage in working with a partner is that in many cases your skills can complement each other in the best way. Let me give you two examples. For years, I worked with a partner named Larry in New York. He was wonderful concerning everything to do with finances, and he was a great technician. For my part, I was good at finding new business and in the handling of clients. A perfect match.

At present, I'm working with David, whose office habits, as I mentioned above, leave a little bit of room for improvement. But that's just for starters. We are also basically totally different in our approach to filmmaking. I, as a writer-director, tend to be very linear and very logical in the way I approach films. David, for his part, as director-editor tends to be much freer in his thinking and willing to try experimental approaches to film I would never dream about. This leads to tremendous arguments in the editing room but also to wonderful finished films. I'm the yin to David's yang, and together we make the perfect partnership.

Do You Need a Day Job?

Whether running an official office or working from home, bills mount up and somehow have to be paid. If you're rich or your parents are subsidizing you, no sweat. For the majority of us, however, there is a problem. How are we going to balance our books? How are we going to avoid running into debt? In short, how can we keep going when clients are not yet beating a path to our door?

The answer is usually a day job or a part-time job, and most beginning filmmakers I've spoken to have done just that. Often, the solution is part-time teaching at a school or a college. And if you teach film, all the better. At other times, you follow the time-honored path of actors and writers and become a waiter or waitress. Sometimes, you'll work on a building site. Occasionally, you become a care worker.

All are honorable jobs but present one problem. They keep you away from your key vocation of filmmaking. This is exactly the time you have to become very determined and resolute. Come what may, you have to keep on pushing your film ideas. Once you say, "I'll work for six months, save up enough, and then get back to film," I think you're lost. Or at least lost in the majority of cases. Whatever happens, you must cling to the idea of your film career and not let it disappear as the days go by. More than ever, this is the time when the fire in your belly has to be stoked for all it's worth.

Depending on your skills, you may be able to find work as a freelance cameraperson or editor. This is particularly true where you've had good equipment training at a first-class film school. Again the question you have to ask yourself is whether that is distracting you from making your own films. And that's a hard question to answer.

Finding Work

Your office is organized, and you're ready to go as a filmmaker. So what's your next step? As I suggested at the beginning of this chapter, you may have made a few films, and they have enabled you to get on your feet. That's fine, but now in order to survive, you have to get more films coming in. You have to become salesperson and businessperson. You have to think of a topic and start moving it around. You have to get it out there and get people and sponsors interested via letters, proposals, telephone calls, faxes, e-mails, Twitter, Facebook, and MySpace.

Your topic may be grandiose and aimed at a network, or it may be more modest and aimed at the local markets. Bear in mind how the markets work and what TV stations look for as you decide where to focus your attention. I suggest this is where you come to grips with reality. You can aim immediately for your world-shattering documentary, but raising funds will probably take years. If that sounds dispiriting, let me add, though, that it has been done.

Michael Moore came to public attention with *Roger and Me.* It was Moore's first film and was funded with the $58,000 award Moore got after being wrongly dismissed by the magazine *Mother Jones.* Moore could have celebrated with a wild spree but instead used the money on a venture that eventually brought him world fame.

The first film of Simcha Jacobovici, the well-known Canadian documentary filmmaker, was *Falasha: Exile of the Black Jews.* After using his own funds to journey to Ethiopia in 1982 and research the dire situation of the Falashas, the black Ethiopian Jews, Jacobovici turned to the United Nations Committee for Refugees for support and also got some money from the CBC's *Man Alive* series. Having taken that bold step, a little while later Jacobovici founded Associated Producers, which has since made about twenty major documentaries and various series.

Unfortunately, cases like that of Jacobovici and Moore are few and far between. Therefore, in the beginning, it may be necessary to lower your aims and focus your gaze on the easiest film targets. That usually means turning your attention to the local market and local funding. The easiest markets to break into are public-relations and company films. Hospitals, other health organizations, schools, universities, women's groups, manufacturers, and start-up companies all need films to publicize their activities and raise funds. While their budgets tend to be low, gaining access to key decision makers is usually relatively easy.

Local public television stations may also provide an outlet for films on local issues, such as saving a sports group or honoring a popular town hero, which would not necessarily interest a national public. Here you may well find your funds coming via grants from local history or arts centers.

Another opening you might want to think about is providing videos for local Web sites. You can also consider getting into niche films. By this I mean making films for special-interest purchasers. A young filmmaker I know started making films about model aircraft, how to build them, where to fly them, and how to create a community with similar interest. In order to push the film, he put a few small advertisements on local TV. He also took his DVD around to toy shops, model-making shops, and local air displays. When we talked, he told me he had sold over five thousand DVDs for an average price of $30. He knew perfectly well he wasn't making the news-headline documentary but felt that the niche films would give him sufficient financial backing to move on to other things.

Using Your Specialist Knowledge to the Best Advantage

Every business—and make no mistake, you are involved in a business—plots ways to draw in new clients and customers and build an advantage over its competitors. The documentary-film business is no different. So what can you offer? Lower budgets because you are a beginning company? Maybe. Emphasizing your convenient, close location to the client? Maybe. If you apply your brains, you'll soon see a few ways in which you can offer a superior package to anyone who makes their way to your door.

One of the most useful questions, however, to ask yourself is, "Do I have a specialist skill or background that makes me the main one to turn to when the client, like a TV station, wants to make a particular film?" This knowledge could relate to an area, a location, a technical proficiency, or a dozen other things. The bottom-line question is, "Do I have something that no one else has and, therefore, turns me into the filmmaker of first choice?"

When I was in my twenties, I spent a long time in Israel doing in films on Bedouins, archaeology, kibbutzim, holy places, and the like and also acted as adviser to Israel television for a year. A few years later, I noticed that 13 WNET, a New York public-broadcast station, was mounting a series that would involve a lot of shooting in the Middle East. I wrote to the commissioning editor, giving him my résumé, and immediately got a job as second-unit director and later as producer-director of two of the films in the series. My knowledge of the area and its customs—and my experience—made me the ideal person for the job. Later when I set up a film office in Manhattan with a friend, we started looking for work that would involve a lot of shooting in Israel or Jordan. We stressed we were the experts on both the United States and the Middle East, had good reputations, and could bring in top-rate films on a reasonable budget. During my travels, I also became friendly with a first-rate cameraperson named Len McClure. Len lived in Hong Kong, taught at a university there, had traveled many times to China, and spoke Mandarin fluently. With this background, he quickly became the director and cameraperson of choice for films being made in the region by the National Geographic and Discovery channels.

Pam Yates, another friend of mine and an excellent filmmaker, started off as a photojournalist. She spoke Spanish fluently and covered Latin America. Her knowledge and background made her attractive to networks such as CBS and ABC. Later, films of hers, such as *When the Mountains Tremble*, about activist Rigoberta Menchu and Guatemala, and *State of Fear*, about Peru, emphasized that she was one of the key persons to turn to if covering that region.

Jim Brown, a New York director-producer and teacher at New York University, knew Lee Hays, one of the members of the famous Weavers folk-music group. Eventually that friendship led to a film, *Wasn't That a Time*, about the history of the Weavers and their last performance at Carnegie Hall. Following the success of that film, Jim decided to concentrate on music films, especially those subjects connected to folk music. The result has been a series on popular music for PBS and films on Woody Guthrie, Harry Belafonte, and Pete Seeger. And I forgot—there have also been three Emmys along the way. If you want a film on popular and folk music, Jim Brown's the name.

Dave Grubin, another New York filmmaker, specializes in biography films for PBS. Marina Goldovskaya, a superb director with years of experience in the former USSR, is the one to turn to for films on Russia. Israeli producer Dan Setton has cornered the market on films about Hamas and suicide bombers. And so it goes on. Jacobovici did three major films on archaeological mysteries. Later, he talked Vision TV into doing a specialist fun series called *The Naked Archaeologist*.

One common thread runs through all of these success stories. Every single filmmaker made him- or herself an expert in one particular field, which eventually brought immense rewards and dividends.

7. Writing Your Winning Proposal

THE IDEAS HAVE BEEN MILLING around in your head for some time, and there is no shortage of them. One is about the writer who grew up in your community and became a world-famous novelist. Another is about three veterans who've returned from Afghanistan and the effect the experience has had on their lives. Another idea you particularly like is to do a film about two musicians, father and son. The father is well known as a teacher and performer, and the son, although only fifteen, has proved himself a prodigy on the jazz guitar. You know the film will have to be shot over a couple of years, but you're willing to devote the time and effort. You are also interested in the members of the Vietnam circus who've made a base in your town.

All these ideas are good and potentially saleable. However, you know there are too many to pursue in one go, so you settle on two of them and shelve the rest for the moment. You are eager for action. You want to get the ideas off the ground. You want to find a sponsor and money. What's your next move? You have to write a formal proposal that will define your thinking and then publicize and get people interested in your project.

A proposal is, first and foremost, a device to sell a film. It can serve many other functions, such as clarifying your own thinking and showing your friends what you want to do, and it will provide information useful to all sorts of people. It will show your working hypothesis, lines of inquiry, point of view on the subjects, and all the wonderful dramatic and entertaining possibilities. The proposal can do all those things, but you should never lose sight of its main goal. The central purpose of your proposal is to convince someone, maybe a television commissioning editor or some organization head, that you have a great idea; that you know what you want to do; that you are efficient, professional, and imaginative; that you have a great team working with you; and that their financial and general support will bring acclaim and honors to you all.

Proposals are also used to sell film ideas at film markets, but I want to leave a longer discussion on that topic till later, in chapter 10. Similarly, a proposal might be called for *after* a film has been awarded to a producer. The next few pages are about the general writing of a proposal when its prime purpose is to get your foot in the door and sell your film idea.

Style and Main Topics

In most film schools and documentary classes, you are asked to write a short film proposal for Documentary 203 or Filmmaking 301. You do this, get a few superficial comments from your instructor, and are off and away. Very often, and I mention this from sad experience, the film you eventually produce has no relation to your proposal at all. Your answer is, "Well, things changed during research." Your instructor grins and bears it. What can he or she do? Give you a failing grade? No way, in this modern, enlightened, liberal age.

Yet, your failure to follow the guideline of the one-and-a-half-page document you turned in to the instructor doesn't reach to the heart of the problem. The real troubling issue is that you have never been taught to write a proper proposal in a professionally acceptable form. And unless you can write decent proposals, your future as a filmmaker will be limited. But all is not lost. Now's the time to gird up your loins (an old English biblical expression that I love for its picturesque directness), get down to business, and learn how it's done.

There are no cast-iron laws as to how to write a proposal—only some good hints and sound advice. My main rule, and I expand on this later, is to write one or two very strong opening paragraphs. Somehow, you have to grab the immediate attention of a jaded commissioning editor. You use your strongest hook or bait. Below is the opening of a proposal I did for a film called *Waves of Freedom*.

> One night, shortly after the end of the War in Europe, twenty-year-old Paul gets a mysterious call at his Brooklyn home. "Paul, do you want to save your people? If so come to the corner of Third Ave. and Fifty-ninth tomorrow at nine. I'll be wearing a black leather jacket and carrying a *New York Times*. If I put the *Times* in the wastepaper basket, you'll know the FBI are onto us. Come another day." Crazy!

But I turn up and follow the guy into his office. He tells me, "Paul . . . we know you were in the navy during the war. We want you to ferry ships from New York to Palestine. But if the British capture you, you'll get hung." That night I say good-bye to my family, and I'm on my way.

Unknowingly Paul is getting involved in one of the strangest underground wars of the century. A war that pits the might of England and its Royal Navy against 150,000 remnants of battered Europe. . . .

This is a film about Americans and Canadians and courage and British struggles to hold on to power as its empire disintegrates. This film is the dramatic story of the clandestine journey of Paul and other volunteer friends and their battles with the British across the waves of freedom.

In the opening lines of the proposal, I deliberately wanted to tantalize the readers with an atmosphere of cloak-and-dagger mystery. I wanted them to ask, "What is this strange underground war? What are these clandestine journeys and battles with the British?" Having hooked them, I hoped they would be intrigued enough to read through the whole proposal and give it some major consideration. A few commissioning editors did exactly that, and it was later taken up by ARTE France.

The hook is fine to get you started, but how do you proceed? For a start, aim for simplicity of style, clarity of language, and brevity. Let's just think about style and language for a moment. You are not writing a term paper. Nor are you writing for a learned magazine. Instead, keep your language punchy and short, and use strong colorful adjectives to add flavor.

Consider brevity. Brevity may not always be possible, but it's a worthy ideal. Proposals for major funding organizations like the National Endowment for the Humanities or the National Endowment for the Arts (both of which have special rules) can run to hundreds of pages. Sometimes, you have the feeling you are writing a PhD thesis rather than a proposal, but these are special cases. Few commissioning editors or would-be sponsors have the patience to read long proposals in detail. In fact, if too long, your lengthy, learned tome is very likely after a few pages to finish up in the wastepaper basket. A concise, dynamic, entertaining proposal written on three or four pages is much more likely to get attention. Recently, I was told by a few commissioning editors that they really don't want to see more than one page. That is particularly true as regards preparing proposals for film markets. At those venues, one and a half pages is the maximum. One and half pages! That's frightening, so aim to get your message across as quickly and succinctly as you can and as dynamically as you can, and then, if necessary, you can amplify.

Obviously, there are exceptions to the above. Sometimes, you simply cannot reduce your great film idea to a few pages and still do it justice. But scrutinize your proposal for padding and delete it; examine what paragraphs could come out without too much damage to your central idea. Again, you should be aware that different stations and different programs such as *Nova* or *Frontline* may have their own rules as to length of proposals, how they should be set out, and what the editors want to see in them.

What is implicit in the above is that sometimes you may have to write two, three, or even four differently shaded proposals for the same project, each time toning and altering the proposal according to your audience. The first, the short proposal, is to gain the interest of a television station and to get a decision maker to promise to give you airtime and some basic support. The longer, and unfortunately often encyclopedic, proposal is to get your major funding from various national councils and foundations. And in between, you will write other proposals of varying lengths to go to all the agencies and groups in the middle.

Sometimes, and probably not very often, you'll take the same basic idea you've sent to one station but alter its thrust to accommodate a commissioning editor with different needs. This happened to me when I was writing a proposal about a nineteenth-century English convict called Ikey Solomon. What interested me was that many people thought Ikey was the template for the character of Fagin in Charles Dickens's novel *Oliver Twist*.

In due course, I wrote a proposal (see examples at the end of this chapter) laying out three main lines for the film. The first was the simple story of Ikey, a convict who escapes from jail, goes to America, then rejoins his wife in Australia after she has been sentenced by the English courts to fourteen years' transportation to Van Diemen's Land penal colony. The second line of the film, hanging off the shoulders of the Ikey story, was an investigation into crime and punishment in England and Australia in the nineteenth century. The third line of the film was to show how Ikey's story influenced Dickens in his coverage of crime and in his portrayal of Fagin. Australian television was interested in all three story strands. German television, however, told me that the Dickens angle held no resonance for them and instead I should concentrate on a story of crime and punishment. In consequence, I totally rewrote the proposal for Germany to accommodate their needs.

What should the proposal discuss, and how should it be organized? Again, I emphasize there are no absolute rules and that the proposal is usually written with a specific person or organization in mind. I usually include most of the following items in my proposals:

- Film statement
- Background and need
- Approach, form, and style
- Shooting schedule
- Budget
- Audience, marketing, and distribution
- Biographies and support letters
- Miscellaneous additional elements

Film Statement

The statement formally declares that you are making a proposal and usually suggests a working title. It indicates the length of the film and may define its subject matter and key audience. Often, I like to commit the idea of the film to one simple statement and the simpler, the better. This helps the reader to see immediately where you are going. If you can't do this, then you know something is wrong. Only a few lines are necessary, as indicated by the following examples:

Wonder Woman Shops at Victoria's Secret. This is a proposal for a sixty-minute film on sexuality in American comics, for general U.S. television audiences. An alternative title could be *Superman Shops at Calvin Klein.*

SockoPixNixes at BO. This is a proposal for a two-part series, each fifty-six minutes, on the historical and commercial influence of Hollywood's *Variety* magazine.

Because We Care. This is a proposal for a thirty-minute film on St. Catherine's Hospital to be shown to potential donors for fund-raising.

Mysteries of Rome. This film of fifty-two minutes, made for world television distribution, looks at the secret treasures that are rumored to be held by the Vatican.

Dinah and David. This film, intended for Discovery *Health*, tells the story of a determined mother who hopes her inventions will teach her invalid child to walk.

Background and Need

In this section, the opening few paragraphs set out any information necessary to acquaint the reader with the subject. They also incorporate the hook mentioned earlier. If the film is topical, then the amount of background information thought necessary might be small. If this is a history film, then background information might have to be quite extensive. Basically, this section lets the reader see why the topic is interesting and why such a film is needed or is of interest as entertainment or information for general audiences. It's your invitation to the reader, the equivalent of the circus barker's "roll up, roll up to see the greatest show on earth."

You must pay attention to the words *need* and *interest*. Many topics are out there begging to be made into films, and your job is to persuade the commissioning editor that your film is so dynamic and vital for the audience that it just must be made.

A little while ago, I wrote a proposal for a film called *Gonna Travel On*, which opened like this:

> It is a soft, beautiful sunset. A van passes us on a picturesque road in southern France. At the wheel is a handsome, dark-bearded man in his midforties. He wears a white straw hat, and his peasant-style shirt is open at the neck. He is singing an old folk song: "I've stayed around, done played around this old town too long, and I feel I'm gonna travel on."
>
> As the van travels through sun-swept scenery, we hear his inner thoughts as voice-over: "I've been on the road for twenty years. I've played everywhere. Made records. Been on TV. But what does it amount to? I've got nine kids . . . but do I have a family? I live in three countries, but what do I call home? Well, maybe it will just go on like this."
>
> *Gonna Travel On* is a one-hour film about the travels, search, and extraordinary career of Alex Jordan, master musician, professional street performer who earns $5,000 a week, a teacher, writer, and former member of the Boston Symphony orchestra. Told in Alex's own words, the film presents the crazy-quilt life of a marimba (xylophone) player from New York who abandoned the life of a classical musician to find fame, fortune, and success as on the streets of Europe. The film deals with three issues: the life of a wandering street musician; his search for identity; and the maintenance of family relations over distance.

My hope was that this introduction would really intrigue TV professionals who had to fill slots, such as *Man Alive*, dealing with the world's strange characters. But I had to show there was a *need* for the film. This I did by stressing that the film would appeal to youngsters facing similar dilemmas in dealing with marriage, career, and adventure, and it would provoke them into analysis and discussion of their own lives. I put special emphasis on the appeal of the film to youth, having heard this was one area where TV couldn't get nearly enough programming.

In *Dinah and David*, I wanted to tell the story of a mother, Dinah, who has a son, David, with cerebral palsy. Not the easiest of subjects, so why would viewers want to see it? What interested me was Dinah's determination that David should lead a normal life and not have his childhood shunted away into a corner. To this end, she had invented various mechanical aids to help David to walk and get and out and play with other children. In thinking about why viewers should want to see this film, I had said that the story of Dinah and David would give hope and inspiration to thousands of other families in a similar plight.

About ten years ago, I started getting interested in the subject of utopias. This finally condensed into a project on nineteenth-century American utopian movements, and I started to sketch out a film with a friend, Brian Winston. We called the film *Roads to Eden* and wrote the following background for the proposal:

> The most sustained and widespread efforts to remake the world took place along the expanding frontier of North America, mainly in the nineteenth century. Literally hundreds of communities with thousands of members were established, and the vast majority of them sought salvation through rigorous and what they thought of as ancient Christian practice.
>
> The discovery of the New World and the birth of modern utopianism occurred during the same quarter of a century. The one deeply influenced the other, and the New World immediately became a place in which tradition and history could be restarted and remade.
>
> The potency of America as a ready-made site for social experiment survived undiminished by failures, lunacies, or frauds for the next three centuries. Inspired by a vision of early Christian life traceable back to the communes of the Essenes and enriched by the monastic tradition and the example of primitive (mainly German) Protestant

sects, the American Christian radicals set about building their Jerusalem. Out of a flurry of activity, major groups emerged: Mormons, Shakers, Amish, Oneidans, Ammonites, Rappites, and Zoarites.

Brian and I took some time to establish the background, but we were making a proposal for an hour-long major-network film, which we also hoped would be the basis of a series. We assumed most people would like the idea of a film about utopias but would know nothing of their histories—thus, the detail. Later, we sketched in the outline of the particular film we wanted to do, which was about the leader of a particular community. When we had finished sketching in the background, we set out our reasons for wanting to do the film and why the audience really *needed* the series.

> In this film or series, we will look at the past in order to ascertain where we might possibly go in the future, for the dream of a better world is not dead, only diminished. Thus a series of questions underlies the film. How can we make a better life for ourselves, our families, and our children? What can we learn from the past about sexual mores, family structures, and social organizations? What do the visions and struggles of the utopians tell us about our own future?

Although I've stressed the necessity to show why the film is needed, you won't have to bother in many situations about that element. Here I am thinking about films in which the entertainment value is so obviously very high that that factor alone will sell the film.

The background sketch to *Roads to Eden* was quite long, but then the subject was quite complex and needed a lengthy elaboration. The background sketch can be short or long. You must ask yourself, "What is the sketch really doing? Has it provided the reader with sufficient information about the central idea and premise of the film to make a reasonable judgment about it? And have I provided enough information to intrigue the reader to go farther?" The background information should be a lure to fascinate the reader, to make him or her say, "What a marvelous possibility for a film."

Approach, Form, and Style

Approach, form, and style are normally defined after you've researched the subject. The research usually suggests the best way into the film. Yet, in most cases, at least a tentative approach will be asked for at the proposal stage. This is the part of the proposal that most interests the reader. Your ideas sound fascinating and appealing, but how will you carry them out in practice? Where is the drama in your story? Where is the conflict? Where are the emotions and character development? This is where you must be down-to-earth. If your approach or structure is tentative, then say so, or indicate two or three approaches you would like to investigate further.

Possibly, the most popular film style these days is cinema verité, or observational documentary, but it is also the hardest to write about on paper because you are not sure what you are getting into. Nevertheless, you have to make the effort.

In *Gonna Travel On*, I tried to define in the beginning where I was going and what and how I wanted to do it. The film would be a journey, taking Alex through many lands, and told mostly in his own words. We would follow Alex on the journey and try to capture the scenes that would best illustrate the themes of our film, which were the search for identity, the problem of holding on to love and family at a distance, and the daily life and experiences of a street musician. We also said the film would have minimum commentary but would occasionally feature hard confrontations and arguments between Alex and the director.

In most television documentaries, the chosen form is usually that of the *general essay* or *illustrative story*, and the style ranges from the pseudo-objective to the anecdotal. In the early 1970s, Thames Television put out a twenty-six-part series on World War II that still remains a classic and superb example of how to make history-based films. What was refreshing about *World at War* was that it ran the whole gamut of styles and structures. One film would be an academic essay, while the next would be highly personal, telling the story of the war almost solely through the experiences of the ordinary soldier.

A few paragraphs back, I set out the background for the utopia film *Roads to Eden*. Writing the background was the easy part. But writing about which approach we should use was not—this was something a commissioning editor would absolutely demand to know. It could be done in essay style:

> The film is set up chronologically as we tell the story of the communities from the seventeenth to the late nineteenth century, from the Shakers to the Zoarites. The film will include all the main communities but will concentrate on the Shakers. It will be built around drawings, contemporary pictures, old photographs, and contemporary footage and will be told through a strong, central guiding commentary.

This may sound a bit dry. Perhaps we could try a story form and an alternative structure:

> We will look at the utopian movement through two central charismatic characters: the leaders of Harmony and New Harmony. These two colonies were situated in southern Indiana. The first was a religious colony founded by the authoritarian preacher Emmanuel Rapp from southern Germany. Eventually the colony was sold to the Scottish idealist Robert Owen, who wanted to found a workers' utopia.

> We will film exclusively at New Harmony, which is today still faithfully preserved as in the days of Owen and Rapp. Besides filming on location, we propose using old diary extracts and the writings of Rapp and Owen as the binding narrative. The film will look at these communities through the lives of their leaders, who could not have interpreted the meaning of *utopia* more differently. However, we will also try to recapture the feelings of the community members of the time.

Some years ago, I was asked to do a film on British prisons, a subject I knew very little about. My first feeling, before I had done any research, was that this should be a people film rather than an essay film, a personal film from both sides of the bars. In my outline proposal, I suggested a film around the experiences of five individuals. The first two would be a guard and a warden, representing the administration. The other three would be prisoners: one about to serve a six-month sentence, the second a lifer, and the third about to be released and whom we would follow in his first three months of freedom. I was sure I could find these characters and that the different experiences of the five over half a year would provide an illuminating and moving picture of the prison system.

I set all this out in the proposal and indicated there would be minimal narration; instead, the film would hang on the thoughts, feelings, and comments of the five "stars." I was a bit worried about the extended shooting time and told the sponsors this would affect the budget. I also told them if budget was a problem, I could cut down the number of my characters and shoot everything within a month.

Here the style and approach were very simple and easy to describe. Another, very different approach to the same subject was used by Brian Hill in his wonderful film *Feltham Sings*, which he made for Channel 4, England. For *Feltham Sings*, Hill interviewed various young prisoners at a juvenile prison. He then turned the interviews into rap songs and had the prisoners act out the songs to play back, against the background of the prison. The result is an experimental singing documentary that tells a great deal about the prisoners and their feelings and is absolutely unforgettable.

Where possible, I like to indicate early on whether there will be formal narration, direct dialogue, or a great deal of voice-over. I also occasionally say something about visual style if I think that will be an important element of the film.

To sum up: questions of style, structure, and approach are complex (they are considered the subject at length in my book *Writing, Directing, and Producing Documentary Films and Videos*). As I've suggested, these are questions you should have answered in your mind *before* you write your proposal. If you haven't done that necessary homework, then the proposal is a good place to clear your head. The sponsor is going to ask you about all these things, and you must have your answers ready.

Shooting Schedule

The shooting schedule is one of the more optional items in the proposal. Include it when time is of the essence, for example, when you have to capture a particular event or shoot within a particular season of the year. For example, you want to do a film about two sailors that climaxes with the Sydney-to-Hobart yacht race. The race is a once-a-year event, so you have to let the sponsor know that money has to be available early to cover the shooting expenses.

You also put in a shooting schedule or estimate in a proposal when you feel you have to protect yourself. This is so you can turn to the sponsor and say, "The proposal says very clearly we need six months, so don't tell me now I have to do it in three. It just can't be done.

Budget

If you are sending a proposal to a foundation such as the National Endowment for the Humanities or the Rockefeller Foundation, you will probably have to provide at least an outline budget in the proposal. If you are answering a request for proposals—for example, if a museum has declared it wants a film to go along with a specific exhibition—then you may have to submit a budget. In most other cases, I would leave all reference to budgets *out* of the proposal because you don't want to scare the sponsors off till you've talked about the proposal with them and had some feedback.

However, I suggest that as you work on the proposal, you also prepare an outline budget for your own interest. This will bring you down to earth and help you to prepare appropriate and realistic targets for your proposal. Let us assume you are doing a film, say, on the history of American engineering feats, whose subject requires a tremendous amount of archive. A few moments consideration of budget will tell you that you are going to need over $200,000 to make the film. Your local TV station, however, only gives $50,000 maximum for documentaries. You know immediately you'd better send your proposal elsewhere, or you send it to the local station only when you need extra backup support.

Audience, Marketing, and Distribution

Like budgeting, any discussion of audience and distribution within the proposal is usually optional rather than obligatory. If a sponsor has put out a request for a film to train factory workers, or you want to propose a film for a long-running television series such as *NOVA,* then you will not have to say anything about distribution in the proposal. But it is not a hard-and-fast rule. Thus, if your film for *NOVA* is about the Dead Sea Scrolls, it doesn't hurt to add that the film could be shown in many museums and could also become a best-selling DVD.

However, when you are trying to sell a sponsor or a foundation on your idea by saying there will be a huge demand for your film, then you have to prove your claim, at least on paper. You have to show how exactly you propose to get the film to this massive public.

Let us say you are proposing a film on a family of five Jewish brothers who have formed a klezmer music ensemble or on six Greek brothers and sisters who have formed a traditional Greek band. One film will be called *The Coen Klezmer Calypso Mishpacha*, the other *The Mykonos Mercouri Marvels*. Both imaginary films will be looking at essentially the same thing, an exploration of traditional music. But they will also be exploring the sense of family, traditions, and for the Mykonos Marvels who've just come to the States, how an immigrant community bonds together. Give or take a line here or there, and some nuancing, the notes on audience and distribution will be virtually the same for both films. This is how it would go for the Greek musical-family film.

Our first prime target for *Mykonos Mercouri Marvels* is the Greek immigrant community in the United States. We will publicize the film in churches and in Greek community associations and newspapers. We will make it available to high schools with Greek students and to universities that are developing ethnic studies. Already we have sensed a tremendous interest in this project in the Greek community, at both a local and a national level. We also believe the film can be widely distributed in Australia, which, too, has a large Greek immigrant community.

We also see wide possibilities for television sales, particularly on PBS, and on the cable networks. A showing on any of these outlets could raise $30,000 plus. It is also the kind of program that fits in very neatly with SBS's community cultural programs in Australia. Museums, public libraries, and university libraries would also buy it for their permanent collections. We also believe it would find a strong DVD sales and rental market among special groups interested in music, dance, ethnic studies, and American and Greek history.

As you can easily see, this kind of template, with a few variations, would also serve very easily to explain distribution possibilities on the *Coen Klezmer* film. The immigration emphasis would probably be dropped, and much would be said about the renewed interest in klezmer music. The notes on family and bonding would be very similar, as would the notes on television distribution and general and university sales.

Biographies and Support Letters

Toward the end of the proposal, it is customary to give a short biographical description of yourself and the other principal filmmakers involved in the project. What the sponsor is primarily interested in is who you are and what your track record is. This obviously presents some difficulties if you are a beginning filmmaker with only a small body of work behind you. You may want to consider trying to get a major filmmaker to join his or her name to the project as adviser or codirector. The known name will add clout to your project and get it considered more seriously.

Even if your track record is limited, add any letters of praise for your earlier work and all mention of festivals you've attended and prizes you've received. Include any support letters from organizations or individuals who've shown a liking for your idea and any letters from any television station that has shown an interest.

Miscellaneous Additional Elements

Your idea is to sell your project and get it off the ground and moving; therefore, you add anything you believe will help people understand and support your concept and get the proposal accepted. This might include materials such as maps, photos, and drawings. It might include the names of any academics who are acting as your advisers. And it might include a full revenue plan if your documentary is aimed at a theatrical release.

You should also think seriously about making a video teaser when you are considering making a long film for television. A video teaser is a five- to ten-minute video that highlights what the film is going to be about. This preview can be one of your strongest selling tools. The great proposal on the history of the Grand Canyon takes on a greater strength when you show the power and beauty of the place. And though your history of the U.S. Marine Corps is attractive, it will get an even better reception when supported by a strong visual backup.

Another practical reason for the video is that fund-raising for independent films is often done at parlor meetings. These are meetings in somebody's house where friends are invited to hear you talk about the film and help raise donations for it. Without a support video, these can be very dry affairs. With a trailer, the situation is different. You can clearly show what you are going to do and how well you can do it.

Making support videos for pitching sessions, discussed later, is very similar but may be harder to do because their maximum length is usually limited to three minutes.

One last word. You may have written a great proposal, but you have to get it seen and read. That requires perseverance and determination to knock on all doors, make telephone calls, send e-mails, do follow-ups, and have patience in the face of rejections because you know in spite of everything, you are going to get this film made.

Examples

When I started out as filmmaker, I tried to look at as many different proposals as I could to see how it was done. I learned a great deal. I hope that some of the examples below will also be useful in signposting your way. This section of the book has much in it and is longer than usual because I want to give you a feel of the wide variety of possibilities and approaches when getting to work.

The key thing to understand in writing a proposal, and something that I cannot emphasize enough, is that you focus the proposal on the needs and interests of the receiver. This can mean that the same subject might require two different proposals, depending on the ultimate purpose and destination of the film. This happened to me a few years ago when I was asked to do two films on the same university within the space of twelve months. The first film was intended as a standard documentary for general television and to fit into a series called Education Tomorrow. The second film came to me as a fund-raiser for the university. The working title for both films was Tomorrow Begins Now. The main differences between the proposals are listed below.

FILM A, THE STANDARD DOCUMENTARY	FILM B, THE FUND-RAISER
A half-hour film to explore the changing university.	A half-hour film to raise money for the university.
Background	
The changing university over the last twenty years. Ideas change. Communities change.	The changing community. Education today. Desperate need for a new kind of university. The answer as provided by our university.
Objectives	
A reevaluation in the eyes of the public of the role and purpose of a university. For general television audiences.	To raise money for the university. For showing to small interest groups and friends of the university.
Focus	
A group of students. We explore their world.	The complexity of a university and the need it fills in a community. Also the future requirements of the university.

Format and Style

We follow three students for six months as they become involved in different social, educational, political activities. The style is personal and intimate.	We follow two students and two professors through a typical day. The film is an overview of university activities rather than an analysis of the pros and cons of the university. We intend to stress the building program and the intake of students from culturally deprived backgrounds.

Narration

As little as possible. Use students' voices instead.	We will use a standard expository narrator with occasional voice-overs by students and faculty.

Technique

Cinema verité	Basic directed documentary style.

Point of View

We view the students as basically idealistic and an admirable force for good.	We see the university as a vital element in our growing nation, an element that must be supported if we are to survive.

Just before starting to write this book, I saw and was thrilled by a wonderful, invigorating documentary by Pola Rapaport and Wolfgang Held about the evolution and the making of the love-rock musical *Hair*. I'd met Pola at a film festival and asked her to let me know how she'd gotten the film off the ground. In answer, she sent me her original proposal, with permission to print it if I found it helpful. I certainly did, so here it is.

Hair: A Portrait of the American Tribal Love-rock Musical
A Ninety-minute Documentary Film by Pola Rapaport and Wolfgang Held

> Once in a lifetime you come upon an idea that perfectly expresses a point in time—a theater form whose demeanor, language, music, clothing, dance, and even its name accurately describe a social epoch in full explosion.
> —Tom O'Horgan, Tony Award–winning director of *Hair*

Hair is a phenomenon. It hit the scene in 1967 with its initial wildfire success at Joseph Papp's New York Shakespeare Festival Public Theater, which had just opened. Less than a year later, it transitioned to an astonishing success on Broadway and helped bring the ideals of counterculture youth to mainstream America.

The American and international productions that followed were without precedent: it was an extraordinary event wherever *Hair* was performed, and the musical was blazed into the hearts and minds of audiences all over the world.

Ten years after its original success, Milos Forman directed a movie version of *Hair* and brought this phenomenon to millions more viewers. The musical soundtrack from *Hair* created hits on the music charts everywhere, with songs like *Aquarius* and *Let the Sunshine In*, and the soundtrack record became a must-have in the music collections of millions.

Since its initial spark, *Hair* has inspired generations of young people with its revolutionary message of love, antiestablishment disobedience, and liberation.

Today, *Hair* still has universal recognition around the world after nearly forty years. *Hair* did perfectly express the end of the sixties. Yet nostalgia for the period is only a part of *Hair*'s appeal now. The musical has a cult following among youth under twenty, who have embraced the clothing and the messages that were so revolutionary when *Hair* made its breath-taking appearance at the Public Theater in 1967 and on Broadway in 1968. In today's corporate-dominated landscape, *Hair*'s anarchic fun and freedom are now as relevant as ever.

A look at the credits of the original Broadway and international productions reads like a Who's Who of entertainment. *Hair* launched the careers of Diane Keaton, Melba Moore, Ben Vereen, Julien Clerc, Donna Summer, Tim Curry, and a host of other stars.

Hair—the Documentary will follow the people behind this phenomenon: the creators, directors, producers, actors, and fans. As an upcoming North American tour is planned, it will track the history, from 1967 until now, of this "curly, fuzzy, snaggy, shaggy" musical theater phenomenon called *Hair*.

The completion of this documentary will coincide with the fortieth anniversary of *Hair*, in 2007, an event to celebrate.

People

What a piece of work is man
How noble in reason
How infinite in faculties
In form and moving how express and admirable

The pool of talent potentially available to this film is impressive. Most importantly featured will be author and lyricist James Rado. From his apartment in Hoboken, New Jersey, across the river from Greenwich Village, Jim dreams of bringing *Hair* back to a North American tour, maybe even making it to Broadway again. He is still an unreconstructed, tie-dyed flower child. Jim works frequently with young aspiring actors in workshops, refining scenes from the play, which is always under rewrite. Jim still has a lot to say about the state of politics and the world.

Composer and musical director Galt MacDermot is an accessible, friendly gentleman who lives in Staten Island, an unpretentious part of New York. He has been married for decades to the same woman and has five grown children. From the time he composed the unforgettable hit score of *Hair* until now, he has remained a most unexpected creative force in the musical. There is not a trace of hippie-ness about him, yet he composed anthems that immediately came to represent the hippie movement.

Other arresting characters whose work remains forever associated with *Hair* include Tom O'Horgan, who won a Tony Award for his direction of the original Broadway production; filmmaker Milos Forman, who directed the unforgettable movie version (1979); "millionaire-hippie" producer Michael Butler, who brought the show to Broadway; and the prominent actors mentioned earlier, along with other actors from the theatrical and filmed versions.

Finally, there is a central personality who is now missing: coauthor and lyricist Gerome Ragni, who died at forty-eight of cancer in 1991. Ragni's artistic talent, his supremely unconventional personality, and the depth of his friendship with collaborator Jim Rado will be central to the film. It was their intense and sometimes difficult collaboration that lies at the heart of their creation of *Hair*, and it was their relationship that fueled its initial success as a play. Rado and Ragni played the leads in the Broadway and LA productions, and they created templates for the roles of Claude and Berger that helped define the spirit of *Hair*.

Themes

[In the original proposal, opening lyrics to *Aquarius* and *I'm Black* appeared here.]

Rado and Ragni's stunning book for the musical addressed, in rapid-fire succession, every issue on the table at the time, including the war in Vietnam and its protestors, commercialism, and conformity in American society, issues of race and gender, the generation gap, mind-expanding drugs, and Eastern spiritual training. All these profound political matters were treated with a sense of humor worthy of the term *Dada*.

The documentary will also show the evolution of *Hair* regarding its politics and its relevance now.

Part 2 Directors' Note

James Rado and Hair will be the fourth collaboration (*Family Secret, Blind Light, Broken Meat*) between director Pola Rapaport and award-winning DP Wolfgang Held, who has photographed many independent features and documentaries. The two surviving creators of *Hair*, James Rado and Galt MacDermot, have agreed to serve as consultants.

The visual style of the film will be in the spirit of *Hair*: funny, ebullient, and irreverent. Rather than a talking-heads documentary, this film will be shot in an active cinema verité style with a lively moving camera. The colors, sounds, and music of the psychedelic era will infuse the film.

Scenes we hope to shoot:

Jim Rado preparing for his new tour: casting, working with a new director and choreographer and with new actors. Footage of actors in various productions around the world. Interviews and footage of working with Tom O'Horgan, Galt MacDermot, Michael Butler, others to be determined. Focus on actors who were in the show over the years whose lives were changed by the show.

Verité of Jim Rado and his tour. Following actors of different productions in different cities of the world. Get with audiences and young people love parade in Berlin, Wigstock in New York, interview, and shoot a bit of verité-style interview following around a bit with the people mentioned above and a few others (Jim Rado, Milos Forman, Treat Williams, Diane Keaton, Tim O'Horgan, Michael Butler among the more famous).

For a number of years now, I've been working in partnership with an English friend of mine called John. When we meet, usually in a pub in

Norfolk, England, called Nelson's Arms, we start chucking ideas around that interest us and that we think could have development possibilities. In one of those meetings, after we'd downed a pint or two, John asked me to write a short proposal for a film about Joseph of Arimathea. The film was meant to be the third in a religious series called *Journeys of Faith*. The other films we tentatively discussed for the series included one on Moses in the wilderness, the Buddha, and some exotic Confucian whose name I've forgotten. In regard to *Joseph of Arimathea*, John stressed the proposal had to be short and dynamic. I did some very fast research and got very intrigued by the story, which I saw as a popular history-mystery, and this was the result.

Joseph of Arimathea: The Life and the Legends

And did those feet in ancient times
walk upon England's mountains green . . .

—William Blake, *Jerusalem*

Of course Jesus lived in England. And who brought him?
Joseph of Arimathea, of course.

—Cornish popular legend

We are in the Holy Land, 37 A.D. Jesus of Nazareth is dead, executed in Jerusalem. His followers have gone underground. Rebellion is in the air. As Roman bands sweep across the land, a small group of Christ's followers secretly prepare to flee the country. They gather at the port of Caesaria.

Jesus's mother is there, with Mary Magdalene, Philip, and Lazarus. But it is the leader who stands out . . . Joseph of Arimathea, the man who took Jesus's body and laid it in the tomb. He takes few belongings but cradles a precious cup to his body. Only he knows it contains the blood of Christ, and history will call the goblet and its contents the Holy Grail.

So begins the strange voyage of Saint Joseph of Arimathea, a trip that takes him and the Grail to the west of Britain, to the founding of Christianity in England, and to the birth of stories that will link Joseph to King Arthur and his knights and even to the voyage of the Mayflower to America.

But how many of the escapees know Joseph's other secret . . . that he has already been to Britain with Jesus in the savior's boyhood.

Shot in Israel, Europe, and the West of England, this one-hour documentary takes us from the turbulent first century to a pulsating, still-mystic modern Britain. Starting in a period of Roman repression and pursuit, the film transports us through a savage Europe to a Britain of pagan sacrifice and druids and to a time of sweeping religious changes.

While expert historians examine the truth behind the legend that Jesus once lived in Cornwall, vivid reenactments and location shooting illustrate the amazing life and travels of Joseph of Arimathea, the man behind the myth, and show how his shadow still touches England today.

According to Eastern sources, Joseph was a rich tin merchant, the uncle of Jesus, and took the young Christ with him on a trading expedition to the tin mines of Cornwall. In the Bible, he is portrayed as a secret disciple of Jesus, the man who took down Christ's body from the cross and laid it in his private tomb. Other stories also declare that he collected the blood of Jesus in two silver vessels . . . the Holy Grail.

Following King Herod's persecution of Christ's followers, Joseph, the two Marys, and other friends flee to Europe to spread the gospel. They follow the route, well known to Joseph, of the Hebrew Phoenician tin traders . . . Cyprus, Crete, Marseilles, central France, and Cornwall.

The story seems wild, but legends abound, recounted by Gregory of Tours and others, of the Virgin Mary's arrival in Marseilles and of Joseph's visit to Limoges.

Invited by a Druid priest to the west of England, Joseph sets out by boat with twelve followers for Cornwall . . . a propitious choice. He knows the area well from his previous visits, and Cornwall and Somerset are outside the territories occupied by Caesar's Roman legions.

From the local ruler Arviragus, Joseph receives the Isle of Avalon as a gift. Here he plants a staff grown from Christ's crown of thorns, builds a small mud-and-wattle church, and starts propagating the message of Christ. It is a dangerous life among hostile pagans with the Romans never far away . . . but gradually England's first church takes root and prospers. In 79 A.D., Joseph dies and is buried in Avalon with the Holy Grail. Later, Avalon will be called Glastonbury.

So go the legends that expand with time. The Grail is supposedly buried in a well near the church. The descendants of Joseph and his followers become the forebears of King Arthur and his Knights. Avalon (Glastonbury) now becomes the resting place of Arthur. The Holy Grail disappears to Wales or elsewhere. The Pilgrim fathers setting out from Lincolnshire make a sudden stop at Plymouth. Do they take the Holy Grail with them to America?

Joseph of Arimathea is a classic history-mystery with local myth and folk lore supporting the strangest of stories. Jews exiled by the Romans are supposed to have worked the Cornish tin mines. Jesus is said not only to have visited the England but also to have spent the missing years of his youth in Cornwall, preaching and building a small church. Ancient stones are exhibited with the Christ and Joseph story shown in pictogram. In Cornwall's mining area, tunic crosses are shown with a cross on one side and the image of a young man on the other. And for some, Avalon is no dream but is situated on the hill outside Glastonbury.

Today, Glastonbury is a modern town of ten thousand inhabitants. In winter, it is quiet but in summer it sports a rock festival, folk gatherings, and Morris dancers. While hundreds of visitors crowd into the cathedral, trying to figure out its connection to Joseph and King Arthur, dozens of others celebrate memories of old Druidic rights in the surrounding woods.

The Film, set largely in and around modern picturesque Glastonbury, sets out to examine and unravel the truth behind the legends. Who was the real Joseph of Arimathea? A gospel writer's fantasy or a man of flesh and blood? Did he really bring Jesus to England? Was he a simple merchant or a Christian visionary with a mission? And in spite of skepticism, was he really the bearer of the Holy Grail?

In the end, the viewers will be left to decide on the true nature of this cult figure and all the enigmas surrounding his life.

Documentaries about environment and community concerns are very popular these days. Often they are funded by local organizations, particularly concerned over developments they see around them. For a number of years, I have been following the development of Melinda Levin's film about sustainable ranching and thought the extremely well-written proposal would be another good example to set out in this book.

Living with the Land: Sustainable Ranching in the American West
A sixty-minute documentary film

MELINDA LEVIN, DIRECTOR AND PRODUCER

DR. IRENE J. KLAVER, RESEARCHER AND COPRODUCER

Ranching and the Race to Save the Range explores various controversies over ranching and rangeland management. The film examines scientific, political, and philosophical considerations concerning environmental stewardship, the culture of ranching families and communities, collaborations among ranchers, ecologists, and environmentalists, and the controversial but often successful use of grazing animals to improve land and water biodiversity. Through interviews, archival images, and present-day observational footage, the documentary also explores conflicts over public-land grazing, the economic viability of family ranches, and the idea of the "Western mystique" currently prompting the conversion of thousands of acres of working ranch into "ranchette subdivisions."

The film sets out to show the possibilities and limitations of making a sustainable living as a rancher. Open rangelands have been under siege. Continuous grazing has caused serious degradation and erosion—a legacy that has pitched ranchers in heated "range wars" against environmentalists. Over the last decennium, a new enemy has appeared on the horizon of the open range: the specter of subdivision and land fragmentation. More ferocious than wildfire, urban sprawl spreads through the West, consuming acres and acres of space. In response to these growing environmental, economic, demographic, and social pressures, collaborative initiatives have emerged among ranchers, conservationists, scientists, and politicians. No solution to save the range can be viable by the efforts of one of these groups in isolation. Degradation and fragmentation are threats to livestock and wildlife alike. New alliances have been formed to deal creatively with land restoration and preservation.

The documentary will explore these new collaborations, most of which are still in an experimental phase. It takes as its guide for rangeland management Aldo Leopold's central thesis to game management: "game can be restored by the creative use of the same tools which have heretofore destroyed it—axe, plow, cow, fire, and gun." The task is to find the creative instead of destructive use of these tools. The film will explicitly focus on the beneficial use of grazing in this process.

There is a present-day Navajo myth that offers an explanation for the many years of desertification and land erosion that community has endured; the plants have simply lost interest in growing. According to this story, when the Bureau of Indian Affairs stock-reduction program forced the Navajo to cull their sheep herds in an effort to improve the land, the exact opposite happened. The plants no longer had an interest in growing because the grazing sheep no longer needed them.

While perhaps discounted as an allegorical tale told by native elders, certain scientific and academic communities are no longer so quick to negate the basis of this explanation. The rapid and radical deterioration of land and water quality in the southwestern United States, Mexico, and elsewhere is often not improved by the removal of livestock. Hundreds of ranchers, many working in direct collaboration with staunch environmentalists, are undergoing a revolution that greatly challenges the commonly held notion that grazing animals are detrimental to the land.

Some ranchers and environmentalists are crafting agreements on environmental preservation strategies despite firmly held political and philosophical difference. On large and small ranches throughout the southwest, biodiversity is reappearing and actually flourishing due to various new approaches that force active interaction between grazing animals and the land. Often, these techniques replicate the movement of buffalo or other native wildlife.

These new stewards of the land, who still defend notions of ranching culture and lifestyle, are turning their backs on "factory ranch" techniques. Instead of spread out all over the range, their animals graze in high-density groups for short periods in designated areas. Where "traditional grazing" leaves scattered, ungrazed plants, this high-impact grazing causes a fast breaking-up of thick plant mass at the topsoil—almost all plants are eaten, and organic material is returned to the soil. Plants that have been gone for decades or longer are slowly reappearing and taking root to hold the soil, minimizing erosion and water runoff. With forage and water present, wildlife returns. These techniques, while documented and readily observable, are nonetheless controversial due to the lobbying power of important environmental and animal-rights groups, traditional ranching organizations, including the extension services of universities and the policies of governmental agencies. This film will examine ranchers willing to step outside of traditional ways of managing the land and animals, as well as environmentalists who have chosen to interact with ranchers in search of a common goal: the reclamation of a degraded environment to come to land management that also leads to improvement of water retention of the soil. In these collaborations, ranching communities have truly become environmental communities, and environmentalists have come to recognize in their former enemies a group of people who truly value the land and animals.

In collaboration with CUBES, the Columbia University/UNESCO Joint Program on Biosphere and Society, we are incorporating initiatives such as the Arid Lands Project and the Malpai Borderlands Group in the film. Both groups deal with the threats posed by landscape fragmentation to wildlife habitats, water resources, and economical and ecological viability of grasslands ecosystems. CUBES is connecting these local groups with people and sites in other globally significant rangelands, such as the Maasai country in Kenya, in order to promote exchange of experience and local knowledge on natural-resources management. We plan to film in Kenya, as well as in Zimbabwe, at the Savory Center for Holistic Management.

The film will be researched and shot in several locations, including the following:

- Carrizo Valley Ranch, New Mexico, owners Sid and Cheryl Goodloe
- Trigg Ranch, Tucumcari, New Mexico, owners Rick and Kristen Holmes
- Jim and Daniela Howell's Ranch, Cimarron, Colorado
- Phelan Ranch, Lawton, Oklahoma, owners John and Tamara Phelan
- Richards' Ranch, Jacksboro, Texas, owners John and Brent Hackley
- Malpai Ranch and Gray Ranch of the Malpai Borderlands Group, Arizona and New Mexico
- West Ranch, Ozona, Texas
- Maasai in Kenya, collaborative project CUBES and Malpai Borderlands Group
- Victoria Falls Zimbabwe; Africa Centre for Holistic Management

Interviews with ranchers will be interwoven with archival material of land erosion, observational footage of community intervention meetings, accounts of scientists, daily ranching activities, and interactions with state and federal agencies and environmental organizations.

This project will bring sustainable ranching and healthy water management to a subject of national and international concern. Environmental degradation is a global problem, and this production will explore various beneficial, yet controversial techniques. The result of this project will be a one-hour professional documentary film production about sustainable ranching, suitable for PBS or cable broadcast. Besides being directed with an eye toward PBS/cable viewers, the film is meant for educational purposes. Furthermore, we expect that the film will be successful on the film-festival circuit. There is the additional possibility of multiple versions of the final film, with some renditions being tailored toward community-screening events or school presentations.

Using the above proposal as her calling card, Levin applied for a number of grants. While Humanities Texas turned her down, the Dixon Water Foundation and the University of North Texas provided substantial contributions toward the film. A few private donors also gave considerable help, while the Quivira Coalition (an NGO) gave quite a lot of money to help with preproduction.

Melinda Levin's proposal is a good example of an *issue* film. Another well-researched proposal/treatment on an issue subject is Steve Thomas's film *Hope*, about would-be immigrants trying to find a place of refuge in Australia. Thomas worked on various versions of the proposal, and below is part of the final one submitted to the Australian Film Commission for their O strand. The proposal was accompanied by various photos, which unfortunately I have had to omit. Basically, Thomas's application follows the form I outlined earlier. Thus, inter alia, he adds full information about budget, proposed production schedule, and distribution ideas. He also sets out his rationale for applying for AFC funding, explains why his film fits into the O strand, and adds statements from himself and his producer about their heartfelt feelings for making the film.

The proposal is long, and I apologize both to Thomas and my readers for having to do some very substantial cutting so I could use it in this chapter.

Hope

WRITTEN AND DIRECTED BY STEVE THOMAS

PRODUCED BY SUE BROOKS AND STEVE THOMAS

The context of this film lies in the events of the dramatic ten weeks leading up to John Howard's third-election victory on November 10, 2001. Those events were sparked on August 26 by the rescue and attempted landing on Christmas Island of over four hundred Afghanis from a small boat called the *Palapa* by Captain Arne Rinnan and the crew of the Norwegian cargo boat the *Tampa*.

Determined to halt the flow of boatpeople to the mainland of Australia, where, under the policy of mandatory detention introduced by the previous Labor government, detention centers like Woomera were struggling to cope with increasing numbers, the Howard government invoked its "Pacific Solution." Eventually, after a tense standoff, the Afghanis were transferred to Nauru via the naval ship *Manoora* for detention and processing.

The government then announced its intention to turn boats containing asylum seekers back to Indonesia, towing them there if necessary. At the same time, Operation Relex was launched with the purpose of conducting surveillance, disrupting the people smugglers, and, apparently, sabotaging their operations.

It was in early October that during the towing by HMAS *Adelaide* of another crippled SIEV (suspected illegal-entry vehicle no. 4) called the *Olong*, that the now-notorious "Children Overboard" incident occurred, precipitating the government into more controversy. This incident along with the *Tampa* are the events most people recall from this period. But less than two weeks later, on October 19, the SIEV that later became known as X because it was never intercepted and given a government number, sank en route to Christmas Island with the loss of 353 lives.

From August to October, a total of twelve SIEVs were tracked, intercepted, and their passengers either returned to Indonesia or transferred to detention centres on Nauru and Manus Island. By the time John Howard was underway with his third term, the boats had stopped coming, and Australia had shut its doors to about twenty-four hundred people at a cost of over $500 million to that point.

Many of those people were families desperate to join spouses who had already been accepted in Australia as genuine refugees. However, the temporary protection visa system precluded the latter from sending for their relatives under the family reunion program. Amal's was one family caught in this situation.

Short Synopsis

"My name is Amal, which means 'Hope.' After our boat sunk, I was twenty-four hours in the ocean, clinging to the floating body of a woman I had never met, sure that my son is drowned, and I am the only person left alive . . ."

This is the story of two women from well-off backgrounds and opposite sides of the world, both geographically and culturally. One still lives in a lucky country and has never experienced tragedy. The other has fled an unlucky country and been pursued by tragedy. Now they are unlikely friends.

Amal is from Iraq and one of only seven survivors of the sinking of the SIEV X who finally made it to Australia. Three years later, she is battling cancer and lives on a temporary protection visa in a tiny flat in Glenroy, which she shares with a husband who has suffered torture and a son who refuses help. Her dream is to tell her story to the world and see all her family reunited.

Kate is a Melbourne artist and founder of Spare Rooms for Refugees. After three years of what she describes as "useless activism," Kate has decided to paint 353 paintings, one for each person who drowned in the SIEV X disaster—146 children, 142 women, and 65 men. She sticks doggedly to her task in the studio of her beautiful Hawthorn home, which she shares with her QC husband and their Afghani lodger.

For Kate, life changed when the government's response to the *Tampa* "crisis" indicated a shift to a more callous Australia. For Amal, life changed when along with four hundred people and against her better instincts, she boarded the tiny vessel that would become known as the SIEV X. These two women are drawn together by Amal's testimony as one of the forty-five people on the SIEV X who lived to tell the tale and by Kate's determined attempt to atone by bringing Australia's disappeared, "the least photographed people in the country," into the public consciousness through a stubborn act of her own imagination.

The through line of this film will be Amal's life story, told directly to camera without the use of cutaways, re-creations, or other filmic devices. The core of that story is the twenty-four hours that Amal spent in the Pacific Ocean, watching women and children drown all around her, being swept away from her thirteen-year-old son, and then engulfed in pitch darkness.

Wrapped around that story will be the unfolding tale during the remainder of this year of Kate and Amal's friendship. Of Kate's attempts to "do something" for Amal and to put her own sense of privilege and guilt to rest by giving account through her art of the people who died, almost unnoticed by the nation, because they wanted the kind of freedom we take for granted. And of Amal's attempts in the face, yet again, of her impending death, to tell the world what happened, to gain a permanent visa so that she can bring her eldest son from Tehran, and to find out what it was that she lost in the ocean that day when "the poor people's *Titanic*" went down.

Concept and Themes

This is a story of trauma and loss. The trauma is not solely about the loss of life and loved ones experienced by the survivor of a tyrannical regime, a disastrous "accident," and a potentially lethal illness but also about the grief of losing one's own country, whether physically as in Amal's case or psychologically as in Kate's.

Having fled Saddam's Iraq and its aftermath, Amal wishes to be Australian because she wants to live as "a free woman in a free country," while Kate—who has that freedom—is ashamed of her country because of its treatment of people like Amal.

This is the story of two women thrown together by circumstance but also drawn together by mutual recognition, despite their outward differences. If the situation was reversed, their roles might also have been reversed, for both have experienced privileged lives in their own countries.

Now Amal has to deal with the "why me?" of having survived when nearly everyone else perished, whilst Kate has to deal with the assault on her sense of decency and the feelings of guilt that Australia's unyielding "Pacific Solution" and policy of indefinite mandatory detention have precipitated.

Kate's response, after several years of exhausting activism that has produced little change, is to utilize the only weapon she has left with which to express herself—her artistic talents. She wants to bring back into the public imagination "the least photographed people in our society"—those who have come here by precarious means from Muslim nations such as Iraq, Iran, and Afghanistan seeking a new life.

In particular, she wants to paint the stories of those who died in an incident that, as Philip Adams has said, had it involved a jumbo jet carrying four hundred people to Australia crashing with the loss of nearly everyone on board, the story would have been front-page news around the world, and the survivors would have been heroes.

Somehow we have as a country expunged this disaster from the national story. Indeed, it hardly entered our consciousness at the time. But the government's hard-line approach on "illegals" arriving by boat, aided by 9/11 and deep-seated national fears of the "other," has caused great damage to the hearts of many liberal-minded Australians, if not to the nation's "fair go" image.

How as individuals do we deal with this situation? How do we make a difference? And how do we acknowledge the effect that these policies have had on thousands of people already traumatized in their own countries who believed that Australia would welcome them?

What can the stories of two ordinary (but extraordinary) middle-class women from opposite sides of the world, such unlikely friends, tell us about ourselves, our country, and our world in 2005? For in their own ways, both these women are messengers. . . .

Approach and Style

As indicated under "Rationale for AFC Funding," the approach to this film is essentially one that seeks to give the characters space and the audience the chance to stop and listen, to absorb and reflect. Despite the tempting array of other characters surrounding Amal and Kate, at this stage the intent is to focus on *them* and provide an uncluttered throughline from which layers and complexity will emerge (rather than mere confusion).

I am not interested in making an investigative documentary on the SIEV X "affair." It's not that such isn't needed, but I don't think I'm the person to do it. Nor will it be an expository film, although I'm sure plenty of information will emerge along the way.

Essentially, this is an account of the personal story of one survivor who was there and one Australian who wants to understand what it means to have been there. Through the interaction between these two characters and their stories, audiences will be invited to reflect on important questions concerning our national direction.

Nor will this film seek to apportion "blame," for this is too easy an approach to take. This is certainly a film about guilt—both main characters feel guilty in their own way, one for not doing more and the other for surviving—but blame won't heal the wounds that they are suffering from.

Stylistically, this film will also be "simple," in the sense that, for example, there is *no* visual documentation of the SIEV X disaster, no photos or footage of the boat, of people in the water, of the rescue, or the aftermath. However there *are* some news coverage and some interviews (including with Amal) recorded after the accident, including a report made for the Al Jazirah Arabic news network.

Nor do we want to resort to dramatic re-creations or other stylistic visual devices.

Rather than use such visual devices, it is Kate's paintings that will provide a strong visual metaphor through the film. So, we will sit *with* Amal and listen to her story. We will give her the space and time she deserves. We will also follow Amal and Kate together, as they try to tease out what all this means and what the future holds.

The film will combine interviews and observational footage. None of this will be "fly on the wall," though. I see each of my films as an opportunity to explore ideas, that is, as a *catalyst*. For example, this film *may* provide an opportunity for Amal to return to Jakarta to the hotels she stayed in before the boat journey and, afterwards, to retrace her tracks and revisit the departure point in Sumatra to which the people were taken by bus. I will be off camera, but I will be asking questions, quietly probing as we go (as is my want, see previous films).

One option in post is a reflective narration from me on the soundtrack. Another is a less-overt way of doing the same thing, that is, occasional use of text on screen. A third is that the film may need nothing at all by way of added commentary.

In terms of quality and cinematography, I want this film to have elegance (another old-fashioned notion!) as well as eloquence, and whilst I am happy to shoot if some urgent situation requires it, elegance will *not* be achieved by me acting as principal DOP! Although the budget is tight, we are determined to shoot principally with a DOP and on DVC Pro 50 (I do have the experience to record sound adequately though, which will assist at times in saving costs).

Marketing and Distribution

As indicated above, the intention is that the first market this film will exploit will be the theatrical market via the renewed interest among cinema audiences for documentaries. Next comes festival distribution, both domestic and international, and then domestic TV (via a shorter version if necessary). There will also be a strong educational market for this film, given its subject matter, and international TV is a possibility.

It will be hoped that a good response on the theatrical/festival circuit will help in gaining interest from either SBSI or ABC TV for acquisition. A focused international-festival campaign will be mounted, hopefully with the AFC's assistance, and this is the kind of program in which Ronin Films or any of the educational distributors should naturally be interested.

There will also be a niche market for this film through refugee advocacy and support organisations, human rights groups, and the like. There are several SIEV X Web sites of different kinds, for example, and the film could be directly marketed on DVD or for download via the Internet from some of these sites, which attract an international audience of concerned people.

Should we be successful in securing full finance for production of this film, then a more detailed and targeted strategy for marketing and distribution will be developed by the producers.

Of course, in the documentary world, things can change a lot between writing a proposal and shooting the film, but if you are sure about the underlying intent of your film, then you will be able to adapt to changed circumstances. In the case of *Hope*, the finished film became much more Amal's story than Kate's, although Kate remained an important participant, and her paintings are of central importance as a visual motif in the film. If you would like to find out more about the way *Hope* turned out in comparison with Thomas's proposal, you can explore the documentary's Web site (search "Hope documentary official site").

The historical documentary has always interested me, and I keep looking out for good stories, different stories, especially unknown fascinating stories that will be fun to do. *Condemned to the Penal Colony* was one such story, which originated over a dinner party at a friend's house in Melbourne, Australia. My host, Helen, herself a documentary filmmaker, mentioned that on a visit to Tasmania a few days before, she had gone to visit Richmond jail. While perusing the jail's museum, she saw a pamphlet that mentioned an English transported convict, Ikey Solomon, who had been in the jail from 1830 to 1832. Nothing unusual so far. But farther down the page, she read that Ikey was thought to be the convict who had served as a model for the character of Fagin in Dickens's novel *Oliver Twist*.

It was one of those moments when if I'd been in a comic book, the light bulb would have lit up over my head. It was a eureka moment. What a great idea. We could do a film about Ikey Solomon, the first Fagin. That night, I Googled everything I could find about Ikey and discovered a riveting, dramatic story about a convict whose passion for his wife took him from an English jail to servitude in one of the worst of Tasmania's penal settlements.

I spent a couple of months on research and then wrote the following proposal, which I saw as a docudrama. What follows is the Australian version of the proposal. I wrote three different ones aimed variously at Australia, Germany and France, and England. Later I explain why three versions were needed.

Condemned to the Penal Colony
A ninety-minute docudrama for TV

In May 1827, a man was about to stand trial in Britain, accused of theft and receiving stolen goods. If found guilty, he would either hang or be transported to Australia. However, a day before the trial, he made a sensational escape from London's Newgate jail and fled to America. More incredible news followed. The man found that a few weeks after his disappearance, his beloved wife had been framed in revenge for his flight. Together with her children, she had been sent as a convict for fourteen years to the penal colony of Van Diemen's Land (today Tasmania). In an act of folly, based on mad devotion and passion, he then sailed to the notorious penal colony to rejoin them and ease their plight.

For months, the newspapers talked about little else. For here was no ordinary fugitive from justice. The man on the run was the great Ikey (Isaac) Solomon, the most famous criminal of his time. A man, who like Don Bradman or Julia Roberts today, totally captured the imagination of the general public.

Seeing the headlines, one young writer became fascinated with the story of Ikey. His name: Charles Dickens. Soon after Ikey's escape, Dickens wrote his famous novel *Oliver Twist*. In it, he created one of the most unforgettable characters in all of English literature . . . a scoundrel and criminal called Fagin. It is our belief that Fagin was almost totally inspired by Ikey Solomon . . . an intriguing idea that our film examines in passing.

In *Condemned to the Penal Colony*, we bring to life the dramatic, turbulent career and adventures of Ikey Solomon, one of Australia's most famous convicts. Ikey's largely unknown story is as romantic and iconic as other nineteenth-century Australian folk heroes like Martin Cash, Ben Hall, and Jack Donahue . . . the Wild Colonial Boy.

As we follow Ikey's journey, we also observe the grim system of Australian and British justice, which took him from his life as a popular and prosperous ruffian in London to a lonely penniless exile in a penal colony at the end of the earth. Our film is also the true story of blind love and devotion, as Ikey crosses the world to save his wife from the rigours of penal servitude—which he would later suffer himself. In Van Diemen's Land, we see how Lieutenant Governor George Arthur's new severely punitive regime falls directly on Ikey.

And in the background we see the figure of Charles Dickens, documentary observer of his day, striding around London, investigating Newgate prison, taking notes at trials, and observing the convict transport ships and hulks. Gradually, this whole panorama ignites his imagination to create Fagin and to locate his characters Magwitch and the Artful Dodger in Australia after transportation.

Using Ikey's amazing story and transportation as the backbone of our film, we move from the thieves' dens, criminal courts, and sordid jails of London to the rocky coasts of Van Diemen's Land. There, where so much of the film takes place, we look at the life of the deportee convicts, the chain gangs around Hobart, the notorious Cascades women's prison, the isolation cells of Richmond jail, and the living hell of Port Arthur penal colony.

Looking for Ikey Solomon

Contemporary portraits of Ikey Solomon, the possible model for Fagin, show a slim, good-looking young man with a dandified haircut. The portrait comes from the cover of the Universal Pamphleteer, one of the many booklets of the time that celebrated Ikey's escape and general derring-do. Under the title of *The Life and Exploits of Ikey Solomon, Swindler, Forger, Fencer, and Brothel Keeper*, the pamphlet presents us with a man whose exploits beggar belief. He is not just a fence or receiver but a man whose gang infested London for nineteen years. He runs a brothel called Solomon's Synagogue. He deals in flash girls with names like Singing Sal and Cherry Bounce, cheats Baron Rothschild, and shares a mistress with the prince regent. Clearly, a man to give Al Capone and Bugsy Siegel a run for their money. So who was the real Ikey Solomon?

Ikey (Isaac) Solomon was born into a Jewish family of nine children in 1787 in Houndsditch, London. Most of the family were involved on the fringes of crime. Ikey himself was one of a gang of pickpockets as a kid and was finally arrested for stealing in 1810.

After trial at the Old Bailey, he was sentenced to fourteen years' transportation. But for the moment, he was not destined for Australia. Instead, he served for six years on the Hulks . . . the moored prison ships on the Thames whose convicts serviced the local ports.

His flowering, if one can call it that, took place between 1816 and 1826. In a London that thrived on crime, he managed in ten years to build up a reputation as the king of the receivers, the prince of fences. Crime was big business. Organized. Managed. Compartmentalized. And Ikey stood at its pinnacle. He had married Ann and fathered six children. He was wealthy. Famous. Owned property. Probably earned over US$60,000 a year in today's currency. Life must have looked very good.

His downfall came when police raided his house shortly after a robbery. Hundreds of watches were found under the floor but no Ikey. He had escaped and stayed on the run for nine months before being captured. Ultimately, he was charged with thirteen offences, two of them hanging crimes, and sent to Newgate jail to await trial at the Old Bailey. Transportation to Australia beckoned.

On Friday 25 May 1827, Ikey made his great escape from custody while on his way to a bail hearing. Various versions exist of the prison break. In one, his father-in-law drives him off in cab. In another, a mob blocks the coach, and Ikey takes his leave. In yet another, his accompanying jailors are lured into an ale house and drugged. Whatever means used, the escape rocked London. Ikey had flown the coop, and the police were left with egg on their faces.

Revenge was then taken on Ikey's family. His wife, Ann, was arrested and accused of stealing and receiving stolen goods. In all likelihood, Ann was framed, with her arrest being a put-up job. After a brief trial, she was found guilty and transported as a convict, with four of her children, for fourteen years to Van Diemen's Land.

Meanwhile, Ikey had fled to America, via Denmark. The news of Ann's deportation affected him deeply, his passion for his wife being shown in several of his letters that have come down to us. In an act that seems to us totally mad, he then boarded a boat for Australia. Driven by love, the prisoner on the run was going to join his convict wife in Van Diemen's Land, just as the brutality of the penal system was to become even more oppressive.

When Ikey arrived in Hobart, he found his children were in an orphanage and his wife was working as a servant for the Newman family. This domestic arrangement for convicts was not unusual, and soon Ikey himself was boarding with the Newmans. Abandoning his past, Ikey bought two houses and opened a tobacconist's shop in the town's high street. Meanwhile, his wife was imprisoned in the Cascades, the Female House of Correction, for a minor offence. She returned home after five months.

Here the story should end happily, with a reformed scoundrel and domestic bliss. But life is not that simple. Ikey was recognized and denounced by a convict who knew him from Newgate jail. Legal battles shook the island. While the authorities wanted the rogue returned to Britain for trial, others stood up for his right to live freely in Hobart. Though Ikey seemed to have won this contest, the lieutenant governor intervened. On 25th January 1830, Ikey Solomon was arrested and put on board the *Prince Regent* as a prisoner, bound for trial in London.

Ikey's sensational return again hit the headlines, as did his six-day trial, which seems clearly to have been the model for Fagin's trial in *Oliver Twist*. Ikey now spent almost a year in Newgate prison awaiting sentencing.

On 12 May 1831, he appeared for the last time at the Old Bailey. His sentence: fourteen years' transportation to Australia.

After Ikey's second arrival in Van Diemen's Land in November 1831, he was immediately sent to the Richmond jail, where he worked as a minor clerk and messenger. Later, he was transferred to Port Arthur penal colony—seen by some as hell on earth—but given a loose freedom after two years. Meanwhile, his family had become estranged from him. Ann had taken a lover and had twice been sent to the Female House of Correction. While Ikey lived apart from his wife in New Norfolk, Ann received a conditional pardon, divorced Ikey, and remarried. Ikey himself received his certificate of freedom in 1844.

Ikey died in September 1850, after two decades in Van Diemen's Land penal colony. He was close to sixty and almost penniless. More than half his adult life had been spent on the run or in custody, and twice he had narrowly escaped the gallows. A criminal, yes, but he was also a man who had risked life and liberty to be with the family he loved. Thus once he had written: "I am determined to brave all for the sake of my dear wife and children, and don't care what may happen."

Isaac Solomon was buried in Hobart Jewish cemetery, with family mourners around. Dickens does not give Fagin such an easy ending. Instead, he puts Fagin in a condemned cell in Newgate, his face bloodless, his beard torn, and his mouth and face burning. He then leads him out to the scaffold, and Fagin is hung. Ikey could well have said, "There but for the grace of God go I."

Ikey and the Criminal Codes

One of the reasons for telling the story of Ikey Solomon is that it opens a fascinating window onto crime and punishment in early nineteenth-century England and Australia, onto the meaning of exile, and into practices that seem to come from another planet.

Twice, Ikey was accused of crimes that could have led to the gallows. Yet, these are just two of over three hundred offences that could lead to the rope, even for ten-year-olds. Until 1868, public hanging also provided local entertainment, up to five thousand people often attending the spectacle. People also came to watch the dying man's last church attendance. The condemned man was forced to listen to the sermon with his open coffin by his side.

When Ikey and Fagin roamed the streets of London, over a hundred thousand people were involved in crime. Self-contained criminal colonies were in East London, devoted to the exchange of stolen goods. Everyone was a specialist, with the criminal profession well subdivided. You could be a pickpocket specializing in handkerchiefs or watches. A cracksman. A lock picker, a burglar, or a snuff man. And the old taught the young, thus while Fagin instructs Oliver, the pamphlets also have Ikey teaching young thieves.

When caught, you went, like Ikey and Ann, to one of London's jails such as Newgate. There was no state prison system. Every gaol was autonomous and run at the whim of its governor, who could hire out prisoners for profit. Conditions were abominable. Prostitutes mingled with the prisoners. Some prisoners were chained, some free. And you paid your jailer both when you entered jail and when you left.

When the prisons became overcrowded, drastic action had to be taken. The answer was transportation, a cover-up word for seven or fourteen years' slavery. An alternative was work on the Hulks (see Ikey's first imprisonment), huge, moored prison ships that dotted the length of the Thames. When the United States declared its independence in 1776, a new venue had to be found for transported convicts. The answer was Australia. Van Diemen's Land was added to the list as a special penal colony in 1803. One of the main features of *Condemned to the Penal Colony* is we hope to show in depth, via Ikey's and Ann's stories, what transportation meant in practice.

When Ikey first arrived in Van Diemen's, the number of convicts was under ten thousand. Though public hangings were frequent in Hobart, most male convicts worked as laborers, and women as domestic servants. By 1836, the number of convicts had risen to thirty-six thousand. Ikey worked in a jail, and Ann as a domestic. They were the lucky ones. As we shall show, Ikey might well have worked on shipbuilding or in one of the chained work gangs around Macquarie Harbour. In the event, he spent a black time incarcerated in Port Arthur.

Charles Dickens

Dickens was also a frequent visitor to Newgate jail, and from his writings, we can gather the whole background to Ikey's and Ann's imprisonment there.

Almost every day from 1827 onwards, articles about Ikey appeared in newspapers or pamphlets, some of the latter calling Ikey "the greatest man of the time." Much of this must have lodged in Dickens memory and provided possible inspiration for Fagin. One of the most memorable scenes in *Oliver Twist* is Fagin coaching his pack of young thieves in the art of being a pickpocket. Is it coincidence that one of the pamphlets suggests Ikey doing exactly the same thing? Can we not see Dickens leaning back and thinking, "Hum . . . a Jewish receiver instructing a kids den of thieves, interesting idea . . . now I wonder what I can make of that."

Though Ikey Solomon may well have inspired Fagin's portrait, we can also see their great differences. Ikey was a success, a well-dressed man, and a man who was reputed to carry a thousand pounds in his side pocket. He was also well enough liked that both newspapers and crowds demanded his release when he was jailed in Van Diemen's Land. Dickens, however, paints a rather different character. His Fagin is a half-starved, greasy failure; he is a man who informs on his business associates and is left without friends. And whereas Ikey is buried peacefully, Fagin is strung up before a cheering crowd.

In Fagin, Dickens perpetuated the stereotype of the cunning and evil Jew. Ikey Solomon was a popular hero.

The Film and Its Method

The challenge in *Condemned to the Penal Colony* is to create a believable and fascinating world for the evolving story of Ikey Solomon. Various methods will be used to achieve this end.

Location shooting

Our major filming will be done in Tasmania, with a small amount of background being shot in London.

We will film in all the key locations relevant to the story, seeing them as they are today and, where possible, how they looked a hundred years ago. Historic buildings are scattered through Tasmania. In this area, which takes up a major part of our story, we will try to arrange to film in old prisons and cells in Hobart and Richmond and show remnants of old villages and their streets. We will also capture the wildness and bleakness of Sarah Island as Macquarie harbour and the feeling of the isolation in punishment cells in Port Arthur.

Use of old prints and photos

We have begun exploring Tasmanian and London archives and have found a treasure trove of prints and photos relevant to our subject. These will be used very widely, together with CGI mentioned below.

Reenactments

Dramatic reenactments (which will all be filmed in Tasmania) will extensively be used but usually without foreground dialogue. We will re-create,
for example, the discovery of stolen goods, Ikey's prison break, and the
atmosphere of Newgate prison. Great emphasis will be placed on the re-
creation of the transportation experience, Ikey's arrival in Van Diemen's
Land, and life in Richmond jail. We will also observe the Old Bailey trials
and possibly Dickens's study and Fagin's last night before the scaffold. Finally, we will try to recruit the best actor we can to play both Ikey and Fagin.

Film structure

Our key narrative device is to have the film basically narrated by Ikey
from his cell in Van Diemen's Land. Here he recalls, recollects, and comments on the events in his life. We find him looking at and disparaging
the wild pamphlets that came out when he escaped Newgate. Now the
time has come to tell us the truth. With this approach as the unifying
element, we go from his cell to the events of the past, come back to the
cell, and then once more move on.

Though aided by the existence of numerous extant letters of Ikey to
his wife and to prison authorities and others, this device also allows us to
speculate about Ikey's feelings, ambitions, and his thoughts about family,
prison, and Van Diemen's Land.

Ikey's story, as mentioned, is set against a wider and more complex
depiction of crime, transportation, and the Australian prison system in
the nineteenth century. To do this, Ikey's personal recollections will be
supplemented, where necessary, by a sparse narration. This will provide
a deeper and more provocative element to the film.

Computer-generated imagery (CGI)

We will use a small amount of CGI to animate the rich parade of illustrations and paintings we have of the period, mixing through where required
to matching location footage of today. At the same time, we will embed
actors and action within the CGI and contemporary footage to provide
dramatic juxtaposition and seamless continuity between past and present.

Sound design

The sound design will be one of the most important elements of our
production, adding a rich subtext of emotional resonance and histori-

cal context to the story. It will include music specially composed for the film, contemporary Australian and English ballads, folk songs, and street cries together with an extensive synthesis of atmospheric sounds of the times—soundscapes of the streets of the East End, the Thames estuary, sea voyaging, and the strange sounds of the birds and animals of Tasmania as well as the quiet and close-up sounds of the night in prison, the swinging of hammocks, and the creaking of boats' timbers at sea.

I ended the proposal by setting out short biographic sketches of the main personnel I thought would be involved in the production but said nothing about budget, though any one could see that would be very high. I also included a lot of sketches and drawings from Ikey's period, which I inserted between the paragraphs. I reprinted the cover of one of the pamphlets that showed Ikey on its front; I used a photo of Dickens and inserted sketches of road gangs in Tasmania. I also put in a drawing of one of the convict-transport ships used at the time.

The need for different proposals arose out what I considered might be different needs of different potential sponsors. In the proposal for Australia, I emphasized it was an Australian story, would be shot mainly in Tasmania, and made a case that Ikey could be considered as one of the great Australian folk heroes along with Ned Kelly and Martin Cash. In the proposal for England, I emphasized the Dickens connection and added the film would work as a special TV presentation for the Charles Dickens bicentennial.

My big surprise came when I presented my first version of the proposal to ARTE France. The commissioning editor told me he liked the story but that people in France and Germany weren't acquainted with Fagin and *Oliver Twist*. He suggested I rewrite the proposal without those references and concentrate instead on the stories of prisons, crime, and convict transportation because those were the subjects that would interest his audience. Once more I went back to the drawing board, so as to speak.

I'm pleased to say the story has a happy ending. The proposal was actually transferred from ARTE's documentary department to its drama department and commissioned as a docudrama.

8. More on Proposals: Treatments and Problems

AFTER YOU'VE SUBMITTED A PROPOSAL, the commissioning editor or sponsor may ask for a treatment. A treatment is a simple narrative outline of the film, normally written when you've completed the research phase. It often presents much more information than the sketched-out proposal but is not yet as detailed as the shooting script. I mention it alongside the discussion on proposals because often it is used to supplement a proposal. In other words, the sponsor or commissioning editor responds well to your proposal but wants a little more detail from you as to how you see the film actually evolving. Treatments are also useful exercises for sorting out your ideas when dealing with long, complex political or historical films. You should also note that often sponsors will request to see a treatment after they've given the go-ahead, and most foundations will ask to see a very detailed treatment once you've completed the initial research phase.

The treatment fleshes out your first thoughts, after research has refined them and you've done some work on structure and the film's development. Its length can be anything from an informal few pages to almost book size (required for some proposals for the national endowments). Generally, the purpose of the treatment is to show and illustrate
- The way the story develops the film's thesis and conflicts
- The key sequences
- Who the main characters are
- The situations they are involved in
- The actions they take and the resulting consequences
- The focus at the beginning and the end

- The main action points, confrontations, and resolutions
- The sense of overall dramatic buildup and pace

To illustrate what a treatment really looks like, I've set out a few pages from the treatment I proposed for *Condemned to the Penal Colony* so that you can see how it contrasts with the proposal for the same film.

Condemned to the Penal Colony: The True Story of Ikey Solomon
Treatment

In May 1827, a man accused of theft was about to stand trial in England. If found guilty, he would either hang or be sent as a convict to Australia. The day before trial, he made a sensational escape and fled to America. A few weeks later, the police framed his wife in revenge, and she was transported with her children for fourteen years to the penal colony of Van Diemen's Land. Out of intense love and passion, the wanted man left the United States and sailed to the notorious penal colony to rejoin and comfort his wife and children.

For months, the newspapers talked about little else. Here was no ordinary fugitive from justice. The man on the run was the most famous criminal of his time. In *Condemned to the Penal Colony*, we tell the true dramatic story of the life and times of Ikey Solomon . . . a man who risked all for love.

[So far we follow the form of the proposal, but then the treatment starts adding different information.]

As we follow Ikey's journey, we closely observe the social and general conditions of the time and the grim system of British and Australian justice that took Ikey from his life as a popular ruffian in London to exile in a penal colony at the ends of the earth.

Ikey's story commences during the time of the English and Napoleonic wars. England's industrial revolution has brought great wealth to a few but disaster to many. Thousands flocked to London seeking a new life, only to find a slum poverty worse than the countryside. The possession of property became all important to the old, landed gentry and new, rich merchants, but with wealth came an increasing fear of a new urban criminal class. The answer to this fear was to transport the criminals to Australia.

Such is Ikey's world, which we portray in detail. Using Ikey's story and his experience of transportation and four prisons as the backbone of our film, we move from the elite world of upper-class London through the thieves' dens, criminal courts, and sordid jails of the metropolis to the rocky coasts of Van Diemen's Land. There, we look at the life of the deportee convicts (70 percent of the population), who, in reality, were building a new country. The result is a fascinating picture of the social scene of the time and of crime and punishment in nineteenth-century England and the southern continent.

The film is intended as an enthralling, ninety-minute docudrama, using historic locations, reenactments, and contemporary illustrations. It also challenges old and distorted notions of penal history.

Story

Ikey (Isaac) Solomon, a handsome, pleasant man, grows up in London in the 1810s. It is a tense time of change. In the Royal Court, the prince regent demonstrates a world of luxury and privilege. By contrast, Ikey's world of East London is one of crime, prostitutes, thieves, and beggars, which we show very vividly. After falling passionately in love and marrying Ann, he takes up the life of a pickpocket. Unfortunately, he is caught and sentenced to life imprisonment on the Hulks, the prison boats that dot the Thames. Here along with other convicts, he lives below decks, chained at night, while he works on the docks by day. After six years imprisoned on the Hulks, he is pardoned and lovingly returns to his family in London.

Here, he finds a changed city . . . a London of new parks, growing industry, and massive displays of wealth. But it is also a London where crime has become big business. In these surroundings, Ikey's genius blossoms as he became the most famous and wealthiest receiver of stolen goods in London. At this point, we vividly contrast the world of the rich, upper-class gentry with Ikey's underworld of crime, theft, pickpocketing, and forgery. Ikey's universe crashes when police arrest him for theft. After nine months on the run, he is caught and sent to Newgate jail, the oldest in London. Here, we get a strong picture of contemporary prison life as we see prostitutes mixing with prisoners, crimes being plotted, and men in chains, drinking and gambling.

A day before his trial, Ikey stages an incredible jail break, which we see, and flees to America. In revenge, the police frame his innocent wife, and Ann is sentenced to fourteen years' transportation to the penal colony of Van Diemen's Land, off the coast of south Australia. In Hobart Town, she works as a domestic servant in the family of a police officer. Out of passionate love, Ikey (a man on the run) then risks everything and leaves New York to rejoin his wife in Van Diemen's Land.

In Hobart, Ikey finds a strange town that shatters his picture of a penal colony. Hobart is set against beautiful hills and a picturesque river, The land is fertile, green, lush, and inviting. Most convicts move about freely, 90 percent of them working as laborers for the free settlers. Others work as clerks, architects, and builders for the government. Convicts mix and sing in pubs with policemen. But 10 percent are in the harsh new prison and penal settlements set up by the new governor. Meanwhile, society life is being established. Carriages abound. New cottages are being built. The only problems are wars with the island natives and the raids of the outlaw Bushmen.

Reunited with his beloved wife, the ingenious Ikey buys two houses and opens a tobacconist's shop with two sons who join him in Hobart as free settlers. Meanwhile, after a quarrel with her mistress, Ikey's wife, Ann, is sentenced to five months in the Female Factory, the new women's prison.

A month after Ann's return, Ikey, still very much at risk, is (as we see) recognized drinking in a pub and reported to the settlement governor. Ikey is still wanted in Britain. The governor, who is both building a colony and running a prison, argues Ikey should not stay free in VDL. After a short court battle, which Ikey wins, Ikey is nevertheless dragged from prison at night on orders of the governor, handcuffed, and bundled on a ship for England. All this is reconstructed in the film.

Ikey's trial is the sensation of London. People crowd the court. Will the notorious but very popular Ikey Solomon be found guilty and hang? While found innocent on six charges, Ikey is found guilty on two others and sentenced to fourteen years' transportation.... to Van Diemen's Land.

Ikey's journey in his convict ship (which we reconstruct) is similar to 806 other convict ships that left England for Australia over eighty years. On caged, lower decks, guards watch the prisoners gamble, argue, fight, tattoo each other, and sing and dance to a fiddle under the eyes of the ship's surgeon. On the ship, Ikey broods and is depressed. What is happening to his family, and where will he be sent in VDL?

Ikey's return on a dark, harsh winter night contrasts with his first visit to Hobart. In the event, he is treated very gently and sent to Richmond prison as a javelin man, a prisoner with light messenger duties who oversees other prisoners and can roam around town fairly freely. Here, Ikey sees farmers at work and begins to understand the possibilities of this new colony. In Richmond prison (which stills exists and where we will film), he mingles with other prisoners, sees them in isolation cells, cooks for the head jailer, and plays drafts with other prisoners.

One night there is a jail break. Three convicts, covering their actions with song, escape from a hole they've dug in the floor. For failing to report the break, Ikey is sentenced to the new Port Arthur penal settlement, which is both prison and work site. Here, convicts work in deep water, moving logs and building boats. Chain gangs build roads and barracks. Ikey, who again is given light duties, watches all this, including the prison exercise yard and the unmarked burial of convicts on the sinister Isle of the Dead.

After two years, Ikey is freed and sent as ticket-of-leave man (semi-free) to New Norfolk, twenty-five miles from Hobart, where he works at an oast house. Again, he experiences the establishment of a new beautiful town, so different from the London he knew. Later, Ann joins him, but he discovers that after being alone for five years, Ann has betrayed him with George Madden. They quarrel, and Ann goes back to Hobart.

Soon after, Ikey's daughter Nancy marries (in a repetition of Ikey's marriage, which we see at the beginning of the film). But Ann's lover, Madden, is there, and Ikey fights with him. That is the final break-up for the family. The wedding points to a new future in the colony for the family but also poignantly points to the final sadness in Ikey's life. The love for which he sacrificed everything has disappeared.

In the last scenes of the film, we see Ikey working in his old shop, praying in Hobart synagogue (where we montage episodes in his life), and then standing in Hobart harbor gazing out to sea. He sees immense changes, new roads, new public buildings. Everywhere there is a sense of prosperity, everywhere a sense that the penal colony is turning into a new world. Slowly, Ikey realizes that while this strange place, Van Diemen's Land, is his place of exile and his final grave, it will provide a new life and a better future for his family. In end titles, we point out Ikey was buried in 1850 in Hobart Town, while his sons went on to become very prosperous businessmen in Sydney and Melbourne.

Film Rationale: Ikey Solomon and the Criminal Codes

One of the main and compelling reasons for telling the story of Ikey Solomon is that it opens up a dramatic and fascinating window into the social norms and developments of Ikey's time. It depicts the harsh attitudes to crime and punishment in early nineteenth-century England

and Australia and shows how a thriving new colony is born on the backs of thousands of convicts. This is the world our film catches just as it is about to change.

Style

Condemned to the Penal Colony is intended as a ninety-minute docudrama. This means we will be blending dramatic reenactments with location shooting and use of pictorial archive materials. Research already done has identified wonderful archives, incredible locations, and historic spots such as Richmond jail almost unchanged from Ikey's time. Film sequences will show how these locations looked 150 years ago. We will also incorporate local events such as the annual assembly of tall ships in Hobart.

The film will be told through Ikey's recollections from jail in Port Arthur, plus the occasional use of experts and third-person narration. Thus, Ikey is seen in jail at the start of the film. Here he recalls, recollects, and comments as his voice-over continues over other reenacted scenes or location shots.

In reenacted segments, we will also hear the voices of other actors. Standard narration is used to broaden the story beyond Ikey's personal knowledge or experience.

The sound design will be one of the most important elements of our production. The pubs of the time were full of music, with the fiddle and penny whistle predominating. Convicts passed their time singing ballads and dancing on the transportation ships. Thus, while we will use original music, we will also make extensive use of ballads, folk songs, and music of the period, together with an extensive synthesis of the sounds effects, from street cries to the creak of ships' timbers at sea to the close-up sounds of nights in prison.

A month ago, I went to Australia to do some research on the film. While there, I met Sue Maslin, a Melbourne producer, who told me of a film she'd done on Dominick Dunne. This interested me as I had long been a fan of Dunne, the American writer and novelist. Later, I saw the film, which I liked very much, which shows the development of Dunne's career and his fascination with crime. When I asked Sue how she, as an Australian, had set about doing the film, she sent me the treatment, which says everything. From it, you can see how the film was meticulously planned, with all potential scenes and discussions very clearly laid out.

For once, the commissioning editor could see what exactly he was getting for his money.

Celebrity: Dominick Dunne
Treatment

WRITTEN BY KIRSTY DE GARIS AND TIMOTHY JOLLEY

Dominick Dunne is eighty-one years old. He is also a six-time New York Times best-selling novelist about to complete his next novel, a special correspondent for *Vanity Fair* magazine, the host of his own *CourtTV* show on the Turner network, and a much-sought-after commentator by Larry King and other American TV programs when it comes to high-profile, celebrity crimes.

Dunne has spent the last six months living in Los Angeles, staying at the Chateau Marmont, while covering the Phil Spector murder trial for *Vanity Fair*. Spector is accused of murdering House of Blues waitress and B-movie actress Lana Clarkson. Spector's defense is that Clarkson, the woman he picked up only hours before, who was found slumped in a chair with her handbag over her shoulder, shot herself—either intentionally due to her failing career or accidentally. Dunne is adamant that Spector is guilty—several women have testified that Spector has pulled a gun on them previously. . . . After the completion of closing arguments, the jury retire to consider their verdict. Dunne expects a quick guilty verdict. The DA's office prays it can vanquish the shadows of the O. J. Simpson, Menendez brothers, and Robert Blake trials, in which wealthy and high-society or celebrity defendants appeared to beat the system.

The personal story that led Dunne to be sitting in the Spector courtroom is a fascinating, humorous, depressing, and uplifting tale, as told to us by Dunne himself. Robert Evans, who knew Dunne from Dunne's former Hollywood days, offers the timely reminder that there are three sides to every story: "yours, mine, and the truth."

Dunne was born in Hartford, Connecticut, to a wealthy and respected surgeon. Yet, his relationship with his father was highly damaging, and even today, he cannot talk about it without strong emotions. As a child, Dunne preferred to daydream about movie stars and concoct puppet shows rather than play sports. Dunne feels this enraged his father, who repeatedly beat him with a riding crop and would call him a nancy boy in front of the other children. Dunne felt like an outsider within his own family; a feeling that never really has left him.

This shy, awkward, and unathletic boy was summoned from his final year of secondary school to serve in the U.S. Army in the closing stages of World War II. Little was expected of Private Dunne or his preppy buddy Hank Bresky, whom his battalion dubbed "The Golddust Twins." However, Dunne and Bresky were awarded the Bronze Star for their bravery in rescuing two wounded soldiers in the face of a ferocious Nazi onslaught during the Battle of the Bulge. It was not to be the last time Dunne surprised those who had written him off.

Back in his suite at the Chateau Marmont (the "Dominick Dunne suite" as Dunne tells us it is informally called due to the amount of time he has stayed there over the last fifteen years), Dunne continues with his life story. After the war, Dunne attended Williams College, where he developed his love for theater. After graduating, he moved to New York and was offered a job with NBC in the new industry of television. These were exciting times for Dunne. The first program he worked on was, ironically, a puppet show called *The Howdy Doody Show*. But soon he was stage managing shows such as *Robert Montgomery Presents* and meeting all the Hollywood stars of the era who would fly up to New York for guest appearances in this exciting new medium. Humphrey Bogart, who took an interest in Dunne, invited him to Los Angeles to attend a party. It was the highlight of Dunne's life to that point, being in such proximity to so many of the stars he had idolized since childhood. He decided then and there that he simply had to live in Los Angeles. Shortly thereafter, he moved his new wife, Lenny, a wealthy cattle heiress, and their baby son, Griffin, to Santa Monica, and he took a job with CBS.

The Spector trial was the third extended sojourn to Los Angeles after Dunne's ultimately disastrous career in Hollywood. He tells us this will be his last trial for *Vanity Fair* and that it has been wonderful for him to have this time in Los Angeles to finally come to terms with his former life there. For several years, the Dunnes rapidly rose up the ranks in Hollywood society. Living next door to rat-packer Peter Lawford, the Dunnes soon became friends with most of the A-list celebrities of the day. After the birth of their second child, the Dunnes moved into a grand home in Beverly Hills on Walden Drive. They threw parties there several times a week, and the high point was their Tenth Anniversary Black and White Ball, attended by Truman Capote, Natalie Wood, David Niven, and all the other key people of the day.

Dunne's producing career also began to take off. After a successful stint at CBS, Dunne took on a role as an executive at Twentieth Century Fox, where he executive produced the highly successful TV series *Adventures in Paradise*. From there, he became a vice president of the TV studio Four Star Productions, having turned down Aaron Spelling's offer to go into business with him.

The Dunnes appeared to be the very model of a successful Hollywood family. The boys were dressed in matching Lacoste tops ("We were even art directed," says Griffin Dunne). After the arrival of their third child, Dominique, Christmas cards from the Dunnes were always highly staged photographs of the Dunne family at their Walden Drive mansion ("The cards were modeled on the Royal Family Christmas portraits," says Griffin).

However, despite the public success, Dunne's marriage was faltering. In September 1966, Lenny told Dunne she wanted a divorce. The divorce was the catalyst for a downward spiral from which Dunne almost never recovered.

Back at the Spector trial, one day goes by after the other without word from the jury. Dunne fills in time by resuming the authorized story of his Hollywood decline. After the separation from Lenny, he begins to drink heavily. He experiments with drugs. Four Star runs into difficulties, and Dunne looks around for work. An old friend, Mart Crowley, hands him a script he would like him to produce called *Boys in the Band*, based on a Broadway musical of the same name. The drama revolves around what happens when a straight man walks into a party full of gay men. The movie is groundbreaking for its day and receives critical acclaim.

Further critical success comes to Dunne on his next two movies, which were written by his brother, John Gregory Dunne, and his sister-in-law, Joan Didion. *The Panic in Needle Park* was Al Pacino's first lead role.... The next film, *Play It As It Lays*, won Best Actress for Tuesday Weld at the Venice Film Festival. Meanwhile, after hours, Dunne continues his nihilistic behavior. Though he won't be drawn on the details, his memoir describes the evening he set his room on fire while high on amyl nitrate "poppers." Dunne describes another occasion when he was using his Turnbull & Asser ties to shoot cocaine and the person he was with dropped dead.

Despite this secret life, a life even now Dunne does not fully articulate, the critical success of his first three films prompts Evans of Paramount to hire him to produce the Elizabeth Taylor film *Ash Wednesday*, which was to be filmed in Italy. From the beginning, it is a complete disaster. One night at a party, Dunne tells a very funny but very mean joke about the most powerful woman in Hollywood, Sue Mengers. . . . Back in Los Angeles, Evans, a great friend of Mengers, calls Dunne and tells him that his career in Hollywood is finished. Dunne did not produce another theatrical film again.

After several years of feeling like a failure, Dunne describes fleeing Hollywood and renting a cabin in Camp Sherman, Oregon. Here, he gives up the drink and the hard drugs and "strips away all the bullshit of my life." Then his brother commits suicide, and Dunne feels like he's been beaten to the punch. Dunne begins to write. He is fifty-five years old.

While his first novel is not a critical or financial success, it marks a turning point in Dunne's life. He sells all his furniture to raise money to live on and moves to New York. It is shortly thereafter, while he is well into writing his second novel, that another life-changing event occurs. He learns by telephone early one morning that his only daughter, Dominique, is in a coma, having been strangled by her ex-boyfriend, John Sweeney. Dunne flies to Los Angeles and visits her in her hospital room. He describes how her body jerks with each artificial breath from the life-support machine, how her head has been roughly shaven to allow for a steel screw to be drilled into her head.

At a dinner party before Sweeney's trial, Tina Brown, shortly to be appointed editor of *Vanity Fair* magazine, asks Dunne to keep a journal during Sweeney's trial with a view to writing an article about it for the magazine. The trial is a devastating event for Dunne . . . Sweeney gets off with "a slap on the wrist." Two years for involuntary manslaughter. Dunne describes the trial in highly personal terms for his *Vanity Fair* article. It is an instant success. Tina Brown immediately puts Dunne on a contract, and she tells him his article has "set the tone for the new *Vanity Fair*."

Further success as both a novelist and journalist follows. Dunne carves out a niche as a social commentator on the crimes of the rich and famous. His novels plunder real-life murder stories of celebrities or society folk he personally knew, and his journalism becomes persuasive advocacy against what he believes are the perpetrators of sensational crimes—O. J. Simpson, the Menendez brothers, Claus von Bulow, Robert Blake, William Kennedy Smith, Tommy Skakel, and now Phil Spector.

Despite the financial success of Dunne's writing, he acknowledges that he is not perceived to be in the very top shelf of writers. He laughingly tells us that he can relate to Somerset Maugham, who once described himself as being "at the very top of the second echelon of writers."

Finally, two and a half weeks into their deliberations, the Spector jury requests an audience with the court. The judge asks the foreman if they have reached verdict. The foreman says they are deadlocked 10-2. After polling each juror individually to see if there is anything he can do to assist them, the judge states that he believes the jury is irretrievably deadlocked and declares a mistrial. Dunne is bitterly disappointed. On his way out of court, he gives an impromptu press conference for the media throng that has gathered for the verdict.

No one, from the prosecutor to an expert defense attorney to Dominick Dunne, seems to be able to explain why it is so hard to convict a celebrity in L.A. Nor can anyone really explain why the threshold for who becomes a celebrity has fallen so low. Tina Brown, former editor of *Vanity Fair* and the *New Yorker*, simply says that the age of celebrity is here to stay. The challenge for journalists and publishers is to determine now how to produce serious journalism through this lens of celebrity, because without the celebrity hook, it's impossible to sell.

We return with Dominick to New York, and still we don't feel we know enough about the private man. Dunne acknowledges that he is lonely at times but says he loves his life. "I was never very good at love," he says. "I've been celibate for twenty years." Cryptically, he tells us that when he developed prostate cancer and was told by his doctor that it was the end of his physical love life, Dunne says he told the doctor he was ecstatic and relieved. The doctor replied that he was the only person who had ever reacted like that to such news.

The next day, Dunne tells us excitedly that *Vanity Fair* wants him to fly to Paris and then London to cover the inquest into the death of Princess Diana and Dodi Al Fayed. He is an energized eighty-one-year-old.

The following day, Dunne's chauffeur collects us at 6:30 A.M. to take us all to his country house in Connecticut, which is two and a half hours away. It is a beautiful, old country home with a living room the size of a gymnasium. We film him there working on his next novel and relaxing with one of the thousands of books that jostle for wall space with photos of Dominick and all his famous friends and family. . . . At 5 P.M., his chauffeur returns to take him back to New York. He has a wedding on Saturday, and then he flies to Paris on Sunday. We are left behind to film the house. As we wander from room to room, stepping around the antique furniture, the tables covered with porcelain, Italian lamps, his Bronze star, and a thousand other collectibles, we are left both inspired by the energy and passion of Dominick Dunne ("He's still on top of his game at eighty-one," exclaims Robert Evans) and yet wondering about how lonely this shrine to celebrity (his and others') feels to Dunne when he returns there by himself and what inner tension continues to drive him.

I Was Robbed

When I was thinking of writing this book, I sent out questionnaires to about fifty filmmaker friends on all manner of subjects. For instance, I asked, "Have you ever murdered a commissioning editor?" Well, you're right. I didn't actually ask that, but I've often contemplated the happy thought. But what I did ask was, "Has anyone ever pinched your ideas, treatments, or proposals?"

We progress, and we get on because of the great ideas we have and our ability to translate them into films. We need to get our ideas out to raise money, but ideas aren't copyright, and even with proposals, we are entering fragile territory. And the reality is that ideas and proposals get pinched. That means you have to be careful to whom you send your proposals and how much information you give away. The more you can make the proposal yours and the more goodies you can bring to the table, the safer you'll be. In other words, if you can show that only you have the ability to make this particular film or that you are so far along with the project that it's not worth pinching, then you are in a fairly strong position.

Sometimes, a network will demand that you sign a document every time you send them something. This document demands that you waive all rights to any claims if the network rejects your proposal but produces a similar film on the same subject. My friend Robert Stone comments:

> Yes. The Discovery Channel does this, and I won't sign these things. Guess I'm not working for Discovery any time soon. I understand the reason for it in our litigious society, but it still bugs me. I just don't do it. You want a pitch from me? OK, here it is. But I'm not giving away my idea in advance. I've been around the track long enough for people to want me as well as my ideas. But for beginners this can be a real drag.

Most of the time your proposals are safe, but occasionally they get "borrowed." Below, I've set out some war stories for you to think about.

You often pitch your proposals at documentary festivals (see chapter 10). Four years ago, my partner David pitched a World War II story at a documentary meeting in the south of France. Among the judges or moderators was a commissioning editor from a big European station. After my partner made his pitch, the commissioning editor (let's call him Joe) berated David for daring to bring such a worn, clichéd, banal story to the pitching session. An ugly argument ensued on stage. A year later, Joe produced virtually the same film.

Here is a note from Len McClure, a very fine cameraperson/director working out of Hong Kong whose work I discussed earlier.

The networks get thousands of proposals. Mostly from wannabes, but more than they need from producers with a proven track record. So usually they take seriously only those proposals from friends, or people they trust, or people they've worked with before, or the boss's nephew. No matter how good your proposal may be, unless you know someone in the organization who'll take you seriously, your unopened proposal will probably collect dust on some filing cabinet. And even if you know someone inside, you've got to offer them more than just a good idea. You've got to bring something else to the table such as your well-known expertise, or unique access, or money in the form of a sewed-up distribution deal. Here's how I learned the hard way.

At the National Geographic, I had a very good relationship with a story editor who got fed up and quit. After several years, she found a good job as a story editor at a major producer of documentary films for PBS. We stayed in contact, and she encouraged me to send her proposals.

Since before the year 2000, I'd been researching the Ming Dynasty Chinese Admiral Zhenghe, who, eight years before Christopher Columbus, had sailed vast fleets from China to southeast Asia and India and even as far as Africa and the Middle East. It was a little-known fascinating story of Chinese exploration directly relevant to today's global politics and an emerging China. I read everything I could about Zhenghe in both Chinese and English. I went to Nanjing and filmed remnants of that glorious past. I explored the coasts of Fujian, took shots of still-standing temples overlooking Zhenghe's harbor, and planned how to digitize Zhenghe's fleet into it. And so the research went on.

My story editor requested more than a one-page proposal, and I sent it with some hope that all this work would eventually come to fruition in a film. The proposal came back with another pass. "Zhenghe is not exactly a household name. We don't think it would be marketable." At the same time, I'd submitted the idea to the Discovery Channel, where it suffered the same fate, probably for the same (unstated) reasons.

I don't remember all the people to whom I submitted the Zhenghe proposal. What I do remember is my head getting very bloody from banging against so many walls. Maybe I should take their word for it. After all, Zhenghe was not a household name and not very marketable. So I decided to get back to the more urgent task of earning a living, which I did best working as a cameraperson on other people's films. My big pile of Zhenghe materials began collecting cockroaches in the bottom drawer of my rusty filing cabinet.

Then one day I read that Lionsgate Films in England was producing not just a film but a series of films on Zhenghe—in conjunction with the very same organization where my favorite story editor worked. Do I get upset and lose a good contact? Or do I play ball and hope to get on the production in some capacity? I tried the latter approach. The editor's responses were friendly. She said she would recommend me as cameraperson. When it became apparent that the folks at Lionsgate had never heard my name, I confronted my friend, who claimed that as a junior partner in the deal, she really had no clout in choosing the production team.

A few months later, on a trip to Washington, I stopped by to see my friend. Back in her office, I pressed her to explain how she could have rejected my proposal on the grounds that nobody had ever heard of Zhenghe, when almost at the same time they were in negotiations with someone else to produce a film on the very same subject. Our conversation got very bitter, and sometimes in bitterness the truth comes out.

"Because they brought something valuable to the table." Her cheeks went red, and she suddenly decided as a friend to give me a lesson in the reality of producing and distributing documentaries. "Films cost so much to produce these days, no one can afford to fund them by themselves. You've got to have multiple partners, and each part-ner has to bring something valuable to the table." Apparently, what

Lionsgate had brought to the table was the lucrative European distribution. They'd also acquired the so-called rights to *1421, the Year China Discovered the World* by Gavin Menzies, who claimed, through some rather-specious arguments, that Zhenghe and his ships had also made it to America. This gave the story a sensationalist element that would also make it more marketable. The only thing I'd brought to the table was an idea, and they are a dime a dozen and not copyrightable. We parted with some false-friendly promises of future cooperation, but since then I've decided I did NOT want to spend the rest of my life as the unpaid, uncredited Research and Development Department for all the major producers of documentaries in this world.

By the way, on the six-hundredth anniversary of Zhenghe's voyage, there was a plethora of major documentaries on Zhenghe by every major producer of documentaries, including the Discovery Channel and National Geographic.

Pinching is not confined to the American and British scene. A very similar story was told to me by Tom Zubrycki, a young and very successful Australian filmmaker.

In the mid-1990s, I made a documentary, *Billal*, about a young Lebanese Muslim, the victim of a racially motivated "hit and run" case. The film follows the aftermath—how his family copes and adjusts to the reality of a brain-damaged son. Inside six months of the film going out on television, a TV drama was made that almost literally told the same story. Wardrobe was so similar to what my characters were wearing that the film I made would have been examined in quite some detail. Ironically the drama was made by the same network, ABC, that showed my film. No credit was given to the film nor to me.

Another problem with proposals, and I am not sure how to overcome this, is when you show your proposal to a company that is interested but basically wants to take over everything, leaving you with only a very minor credit. This happened to an Australian student of mine. Joanna took her proposal to a large company. They loved it but told her she alone could never push it through SBS television. She concurred with their judgment. The company took the proposal to a TV station that accepted it in a flash. Joanna then was basically pushed aside and almost ignored as the production proceeded, finishing up with an inferior production role and very little cash to show for her efforts. Should she have submitted the proposal by herself? I am inclined to think so. Or at least with an accredited friend she could trust. Failing that, I would have pushed for a better deal from the production company before handing over the proposal.

Here, Joanna felt she was forced to assign her original idea before the production could move forward. Tom Zubrycki also gave me a comment on this situation as well.

> I think this [assignation of ideas] is the norm for people who are starting out in the industry and badly want to make a film. They assign rights to established companies. However, there is nothing to stop them demanding a reversion clause, that is, the copyright goes back to the originator of the idea after the producer discharges all their obligations under the PIA, such as, exploiting marketing rights. So the assignation would be around five to seven years, which is not a bad outcome. Alternatively, make the film yourself—get it to rough cut, get a broadcaster interested, and you get to keep ownership of your idea.

9. Budgeting for Survival and Profit

"OK," I CAN HEAR YOU SAYING. "Budgeting for profit I can understand. But for survival? What on earth does he mean?" The answer is simple. Make some serious mistakes on a few budgets, and not only will your dreams of wine, romance, and a holiday in Acapulco vanish but you'll also finish up in the street, watching the bailiffs haul away all the expensive equipment you bought just four months ago. Budgets are a two-edged weapon. Handle them well, and they'll protect you in most situations. Ignore them, or treat them casually, and they can turn round and deal you a body blow.

Alright, let me discuss this more gently. In order to get ahead, to make a profit as an independent filmmaker, you've got to learn all the ins and outs of budgets. At a university or film school or while working for someone else, you haven't had to think about money in any serious way. Money has been that vague element you didn't have to worry about. But now your life is moving on. You are going to make films whose expenses can range from $30,000 to $300,000 or more. If your proposal gets accepted, you are going to enter into a contract and sign your life away under a formal legal agreement. That means you are going to undertake heavy responsibilities and have to budget your film very carefully. If you don't budget carefully, not only will you not be able to make a decent film and be unable to complete it but you may also be left with very extensive debts. So learning how to draw up a full and careful budget, guarding against all contingencies, is one of the most necessary skills you have to acquire to get ahead.

In reality, you will have thought about the production budget, at least in a general way, from your first moments in considering the film. But now is the moment of truth. My own procedure is as follows. After doing the proposal and before sending it out, I sketch out a rough outline budget, trying to cover all contingencies and get a general sense of the cost of the film. This will all change as I develop the script, but it's useful as a starting point. It gives me a basic idea of the rough needs of the budget, and I am much less likely to make mistakes as I negotiate terms with the sponsor.

The Budget

In budgeting, we often face a number of conundrums. How do you do a budget when you haven't done the main research or prepared an outline script? Do you budget according to script, or do you script according to budget? For example, in a film I'm doing at the moment, a docudrama, I know there is no way I can raise above a certain amount and, therefore, have had to omit certain scenes from the script. Do you budget according to what you know the sponsor can afford, or do you budget in the hope you can raise the funds from different sources and, therefore, don't limit the script? There is no absolute answer to these questions, as the conditions under which you make each film will be different.

Only one thing is vital: your budget must be as complete and as accurate as possible. If you make a mistake in your budgeting and commit yourself to make a film for what turns out to be an unrealistic sum, you are likely to finish up bankrupt or at least in a very sorry financial situation. A friend of mine, a great filmmaker but no financial wizard, committed himself and his company to do a film for CBS on the mayors of New York. They gave him a budget of $100,000 and told him that was the limit. The film cost him $130,000. You can draw your own conclusions.

My answer to these problems is to put into the budget every single item I think I'll need and then a few more; I always overbudget rather than underbudget, though not all filmmakers agree with this attitude. I believe in being safe rather than sorry. You may lose a few films if you are bidding in a competitive situation, but it's worth it in the end. A decent budget will save you many a sleepless night.

The only time when I might consciously underbudget is when I'm angling for a new long-term client. In that situation, which promises many films in the future, I may deliberately be willing to take a loss in the hope that the client will bring me many better deals later on.

Below are the major items that appear in most films and video budgets; this list should serve as a good first guide. If something occurs to you that does not appear here, then add it, as you'll probably need it.

A. Research
1. Script research, including travel and hotels, books, photocopies, library viewing expenses, research assistants
2. General preproduction expenses, including travel, meetings, and the like

B. Shooting
1. Crew
   Cameraperson
   Assistant cameraperson
   Sound person
   Lighting technician
   Production assistant
   Driver and/or grip
   Production manager
   Line producer
   Makeup artist
   Teleprompter operator
2. Equipment
   Camera and usual accessories
   Special camera equipment, such as fast lenses and underwater rigs
   Tape recorders and microphones
   Lighting
   Teleprompter
3. Location expenses
   Vehicle rental
   Gasoline
   Helicopter or boat hire
   Crew food
   Hotels
   Airfares
   Location shooting fees
4. Stock
   Negative film
   Tape cassettes

Developing film and making work print

Tape reels and audio cassettes

Magnetic tape, including transfers

Leader and spacing

C. Postproduction

  1. Editing

  Editor

  Assistant editor

  Sound editor

  Editing-room supplies and equipment, including video offline

  2. Lab and other expenses

  Sound coding

  Sound designer

  Music and sound transfers

  Opticals and special effects

  Computer generated images (CGIs)

  Video window dubs

  Making titles

  Narration recording

  Sound mix

  Negative cutting

  Making optical negative

  First and second answer prints

  Making video master

  Online video editing

  Release prints—theater, television, videocassette dubs, and the like

  Making DVDs

  3. General

  Office expenses, rent, telephone, faxes, photocopying, and the like

  Messengers

  Transcripts

  Music, photo, and archive royalties

  Errors and omissions (E & O) insurance

  Insurance

  Legal costs

  Dispatch and customs clearance

  Voice-overs

  Translations

  Advertising and publicity

Payroll-tax provisions
4. Personnel
 Writer
 Director
 Producer
 Narrator
 Associate producer
 Researcher
 General assistant
D. Sponsor-station overheads
E. Company provisions
 1. Contingency
 2. Company profit

Eighty percent of the above items occurs in most documentaries. The other 20 percent depends on the size and finances of the production. If the production is small, there may be no line producer or production manager or general assistant. Almost certainly, there will be no makeup artist. And you'll probably find that not only are you writing and directing but also doing all the producing and research.

Two notes. First, the crew is normally budgeted at a daily rate and the editor and assistant per week. The cameraperson might appear on the budget for fourteen days at $300 per day, while the editor would be written in for ten weeks at $1,000 per week. Equipment rental is also budgeted per day, though some renters will give you six days' hire for the price of five. Very often, the cameraperson will be hired with his or her own camera. Ditto the soundperson. The second thing to note is that stock, both film and magnetic-sound stock, is usually estimated at so-many-cents per foot—for example, twenty thousand feet of film stock at $0.18 per foot.

Besides the above, a few items occur from time to time, and they are worth noting in your check list:

- graphic design
- studio use
- actors
- special wardrobe
- special props
- donations, entertainment, and presents

If you are shooting a docudrama, with the emphasis more on drama than documentary, you'll probably also need to reference a drama budget to see what extra items you should add.

At the end of this chapter are examples of three budgets. One is a high-end budget for an hour film on a national television network that requires a lot of shooting abroad and extensive use of archives. The second budget is also for an hour film but one made on a much more modest scale. Finally, the third budget is for a very low-cost public-relations film.

Most of the items above in both the main and miscellaneous lists are obvious, but others require some explanation because a miscalculation about them can have grave effects on the budget.

Stock and Ratios

It is extremely important to try to estimate at the start of your production how much film stock or how many tapes you are likely to require for your shoot. A film that can be preplanned to the last detail and has fairly easy shooting may require a ratio of only six to one—that is, if you want a half-hour final film, you need to shoot only three hours of film. A more complex film, however, with masses of interviews may require a ratio of twelve or fourteen to one, which is fairly standard for major-television documentaries. If you are going for verité, emulating the films of the early observational pioneers like Fred Wiseman, Ricky Leacock, Don Pennebaker, or David Maysles and Albert Maysles, then you may be in for a shooting ratio of thirty or forty to one.

At this moment of writing, it costs over $400 to produce a twenty-minute-film work print. This is not cheap and is a warning to you to figure out very carefully what ratio you will be using; otherwise, your budget will be terribly inaccurate. With the lower costs of videocassettes and DVDs, you can afford to give yourself more leeway, but even then you should be very careful with your estimates. Generally, I budget on a ratio of ten to one if most of the shooting can be well planned and thought out in advance.

Equipment

Many people own their own equipment, which is much more feasible now than ten years ago. With a partner, I share two cameras (costing under $7,000 each) and two editing computers and screens. That is usually more than adequate for the kind of jobs we undertake. Where the needs get more specialized, I rent, always looking for the best deal. However, even if you own your own equipment, you should state a cost for it in the budget. This helps you at the end of the year to assess whether the equipment is really paying for itself.

Crew and Shooting Time

One reason for writing a decent script or a full treatment before shooting is that it helps in predicting the shooting days needed. These days, the minimum cost for a full film crew, including production manager, driver, and rented equipment, is about $1,500 a day. For the best cameraperson and the fanciest equipment, costs may go up to $2,500 a day. If you have underestimated the number of days needed for shooting, you will be spending anywhere between $1,500 and $2,500 out-of-pocket per day. So again, overestimate rather than underestimate.

If you are doing your own shooting and work with minimum crew (and you drive and make the crew sandwiches yourself), then obviously your daily costs will be much lower than above. But even in that situation, you should get in the habit of making a good approximate estimate of shooting time.

Be sure, also, that you know exactly what you've agreed with the crew. Is the arrangement for eight, ten, or twelve hours per day? Can you make a buyout arrangement, offering them a flat fee whatever the length of the shooting day? What arrangements have you made with them regarding traveling time, both before and after they've finished work? If the cameraman has to travel an hour to meet you on location, is that hour within his daily rate, or do you have to pay extra? Are you going to pay the crew on their days off, when they are not shooting but have to be away from home? Do you have to deal with a union? What are you paying for a location scout? These questions must be resolved before you go out to shoot; otherwise, you will think you are paying one rate but may end up with an unexpectedly inflated bill at the end of the day.

The problem, which you've seen immediately, is that you are dealing with a lot of imponderables. The only useful guideline, then, is to err on the generous side. This is also true about editing, as it is often impossible to say whether the editing will take eight weeks or ten.

Where does the sponsor come into all this? I usually agree with the sponsor about the number of shooting days and editing weeks, which I then put into the budget, but try to get the sponsor also to agree to pay extra if shooting gets extended for the best of reasons. This approach is discussed at greater length in the section on the production contract.

CGIs

Computer-graphic images are being employed more and more in documentary films, particularly in docudramas and films dealing with history. I don't particularly like CGIs, finding all the black, stormy skies a bit fake, but many commissioning editors have fallen in love with this new technology. That's fine, but you must note that CGIs are very expensive, so budget accordingly.

If you do think you might need CGIs or special effects, the best thing to do is talk to a special-effects house. Ask for a demonstration, which they'll love to give you. Explain the film you're doing and the limits of your budget, and see how they can help you at a reasonable price. I've found many of these shops and studios to be hungry for work and accordingly very accommodating on costs.

Graphic Design

It's become more and more fashionable to employ some fancy graphic designs in your credits or in the body of the work itself to jazz up your film. In the past, purists frowned upon this. Today, the attitude seems to be "what works for James Bond films can work for us." In the last week alone, I've seen two films that use some imaginative graphics to bolster the message. One was an archaeology film by Simcha Jacobovici in which ancient battles between Israelites and Palestinians are staged by Lego figures. In another film about corporate battles and company takeovers, the shenanigans and scheming of the banks, financiers, and corporate raiders are all played out by pieces on a monopoly board. In Agnieszka Piotrowska's fascinating film *The Bigamists*, playing-card figures simulate the emotions of couples involved in deception and bigamy, all to very good effect.

All three films were fun. Used wisely, there is no doubt that good graphic designs can immeasurably enhance a film. But graphics are expensive. So be warned!

Music, Photo, and Archive Royalties

When I was preparing this book, I wrote to an American producer friend, Robert Stone, for his thoughts on copyright. Robert had just finished an excellent film on Patty Hearst and was preparing another one to be called *Hollywood Vietnam*. This was his reply: "Copyright fees are insane and make me want to give up this whole business entirely. Particularly as I've spent the better part of my career making heavily archival films."

Well, there you have a producer's view in a nutshell, a view I heavily endorse. Copyright payments are a pain, but they have to be reckoned in to the budget. Copyright payments may be necessary for the use of recorded library music, certain photographs, and film archives. Most of the time that you use ready-made recordings, you will have to pay a fee to the company that made the recording. The fee is usually based on the length of the selection you use, the geographic areas where the film will be shown, and the type of audience for whom the film is intended. The rate for theatrical use or commercial television use is usually higher than for educational purposes. Occasionally, you may be able to arrange for the free use of a piece of music if the film is for public-service purposes.

If you are unsure of the final use of the film, its best to negotiate the rights you want and fix a sum that will be payable if you alter the use. My policy is to get everything fixed in one go before the film is made; if you try to negotiate later, and the seller knows you badly want the rights, you are in a bad bargaining position. In other words, make a provisional clearance that will stand you in good stead later if you need it.

Music fees can be very high, so you often look for alternatives. Given the advance of computer music programs, it may often be cheaper to have music specially composed for your film than to use a library recording. You may also find, with a bit of hunting, that the music you want was recorded before certain copyright rules were in force. In one film, I used some Russian folk music that had been recorded in the twenties and was outside copyright legislation.

The position with photographs is slightly different. If the photographs are not in public domain, you will have to make an arrangement with each individual photographer. Newspapers are usually fairly good at letting you use photographs for a small fee, whereas individual photographers will be much more expensive. It makes sense to hunt around for options on different photographs or to find photographs in the public domain. The extra trouble may save considerable sums later.

Besides photos, you may want some general images for your film, such as posters or advertisements. These days, to find many of these items, we turn to Google Images or some such similar search engine. When I was doing a film on Joseph Stalin, Google turned up some propaganda posters of Stalin during World War II. However, look very carefully at these images. Many will be in the public domain. Others will still be under copyright. If so, you must contact the copyright owner and negotiate a fee.

And that's the golden rule. To avoid trouble, obtain permission before use. I know that many people don't. They pinch from everyone and pay nothing. It seems a stupid policy, one that ultimately works against the film and the director. On the one hand, you lay yourself open to a law suit, and on the other, you may find that a television station will not accept a film unless you can produce written copyright permissions.

Most of the above comments also apply to stock footage or film archive rights. Like music and photos, the cost of the rights will vary according to the purpose and destination of the film. For years, and I'm talking about the situation till the midseventies, most archive rights were comparatively cheap; battle footage from World War II could be had for a few dollars a foot. Today, though, film archives have turned into big business, demanding immense sums for archival clips. It is not unusual to find and archive asking $50 to $60 for a final used foot; this translates to $100 for three seconds in a completed film, or $2,000 to $3,000 per minute of screen time. If your film deals with history or a well-known personality, you may have to budget in a huge sum to cover archive rights. In a film I did about World War II for a New York educational station, our archive payments came to more than $30,000.

Part of the answer is to hunt for film in the public domain, such as film held by the National Archives in Washington, D.C. Where this is not possible and where people are not willing to charge you just a nominal sum because your film is so great and they like your face, you just have to budget adequately.

Even though archives usually publish a price per foot or per minute for their material, you may find it helps to talk personally to the management or big boss. If the high-ups like your film, they may arrange for you to have the rights at a reduced cost. You don't lose anything by talking. Sometimes, the management will acknowledge that beginning filmmakers aren't millionaires or big television corporations and make allowances. They also may think that although you don't have much money now, you may hit the success trail in a year or so, and it would be nice to have you as a client. The discussions don't always pay off, but they're worth a try.

In negotiating use of rights, you must remember that the price may vary according to territories demanded and length of use. The price of rights for the United States alone and for three years will probably be less than for worldwide rights for ten years. You must also consider final use. Do you want rights merely for festival showings or also for television, cinemas, home video, educational purposes, DVDs, and so on? The rule is to make sure you've acquired the rights for what you need.

You should also look at alternative sources for your material. Basically, the same material may exist in different archives and at different prices. Two years ago, I needed material on World War II and on British warships operating off the Palestinian coast. I found practically the same material in two British archives. One, however, was considerably cheaper than the other, and that's where I went. I should also add the service was better, and they were also willing to make concessions on price.

Having covered all the above, I should mention there has been a growing rebellion against the exorbitant costs being demanded these days for rights. This rebellion has been translated into action by academics such as Pat Aufderheide and others, working out of the Center for Social Media at the American University, Washington, D.C. Their basic argument is that in many cases, payment for rights is unnecessary. The basis for their argument is the evolution of a new legal doctrine called "fair use." You can read more about this in a paper available on the Web called "The Documentary Filmmakers' Statement of Best Practices in Fair Use." In a recent publicity update, the center cites a number of films that could not have been seen publicly or possibly even finished without the use of the new doctrine. These films include *The Trials of Darryl Hunt*, *Hip Hop: Beyond Beats and Rhymes*, and *Wanderlust*. The center also claims that a number of PBS stations have also incorporated the doctrine of fair use into their business practices.

The terrain as yet is rocky and unclear. For more on what is happening in copyright and when and when not to pay, I would strongly recommend Michael Donaldson's excellent book *Clearance and Copyright*.

Two final comments on the subject. Whereas fair use may well justify your use of some archive material, your real problem may be getting hold of the material in the first place. If it's only available from one source who wants money, you are screwed. Secondly, if you use what seems to be copyrighted material in your films, citing fair use, you may still finish up being sued. So the question is, do you have the money to defend yourself?

Errors and Omissions Insurance

Errors and omissions insurance, or E & O insurance, as it is generally called, basically insures the filmmaker against being sued for breach of copyright or for libel or slander of someone in the film. It provides payment for a legal defense against a court action. However, it is very expensive and can cost between $5,000 and $8,000 to purchase for a one-hour film. While the need for E & O insurance is usually ignored in films made for Europe, it will be demanded by all U.S. and Canadian broadcasters in coproductions and film purchases. The way out of this expensive demand is to get the big coproducer to foot this bill. Sometimes this works, sometimes it doesn't, but there is no harm in asking. For those interested, a very good discussion of the whole nature of E & O insurance is in Donaldson's book cited above.

The strange thing about E & O insurance is it's something every TV station calls for but is very rarely used. There is a sense that if you actually have to call on the insurance, the stations won't trust you to make a film for them again. What I personally do is leave E & O insurance till it's absolutely necessary. That means if I make a film for Europe or the United Kingdom, I don't take out that insurance. But if I then get a sale to the United States, I'll take it out, since the sale payment will offset the insurance costs.

General Insurance

We have insurance because of Murphy's Law: what can go wrong, will go wrong. Having insurance helps you face chaos and catastrophe with a certain equanimity. Insurance should cover equipment, stock, crew, properties, and third-party risk. It should also cover office and equipment, E &O mentioned above, and general liability. Within reason, your coverage should be as wide as possible. You should insure the film through the shooting and up to the making of a master negative or master cassette. You should also pay attention to faulty equipment or damage arising during processing or video editing. The usual compensation covers the cost of reshooting.

However, insurance will not cover faulty original film stock or bad cassettes. Therefore, be absolutely certain to test your stock before shooting. Nor will insurance cover damage or fogging by airport X-rays. Insurance used to cover these things, but most companies have now deleted such coverage. The only answer is to have the film handchecked (not always possible) and/or carry the film in lead-lined bags. Most airport authorities seem to be aware these days of the dangers of X-rays to film stock, and most machines state that they are safe for film up to 1000 ASA. That may be so, but my heart always trembles until I see a processed film without damage.

I always insure sets and properties as well as film equipment. You should also insure yourself to cover workers' compensation. This provides medical, disability, and death benefits to any member of the crew who becomes injured while working for you. You can argue they are independent contractors and therefore outside your responsibility, but fewer and fewer people accept this as lessening the responsibility. You also need to cover third-party risk in case the filming damages any property or any person. I didn't get this coverage till one day my lights melted a plastic roof and almost set a school on fire. That was the only lesson I needed.

Most insurance companies these days are unwilling to insure one individual film, preferring to work only on a yearly base. The answer is a cooperative in which the insurance costs can be shared among various friends who between them will have various films being shot during the year.

Translations

Though you are probably making your original film in English, you may sometimes also find yourself shooting abroad and interviewing in a foreign language. If you think this is indeed a possibility, then you should allow for translation services in your budget. In *Fahima's Story*, although K-Rahmer's film was intended for Australian audiences, half the film was shot in Farsi, with translations taking up a big part of the cost. If you think your film has international appeal, you may also want to make translations for sale abroad. This, too, has to find a place in your costing.

Advertising and Publicity

Filmmakers often forget to allow for postproduction advertising and publicity. The completion of the film itself is only part of the process. Later, you will want to enter it into film festivals, make advertising and publicity brochures, and take the film to various film markets. You will also want to make a publicity package to send to newspapers, magazines, and TV stations, including a DVD of the film for prebroadcast viewing. You may even want to employ a publicity agent to get news of your film into the newspaper gossip columns and on TV. All these items require money, so make sure an allowance for them appears in the budget.

Legal Matters

At some point in the film, either in the negotiations with the sponsor or later, you may need to seek legal advice. This becomes particularly important if you are involved in a coproduction or a foreign sale or want to take an option on a book or an article that looks like a good basis for a documentary. You may want a lawyer to go over your film, in certain situations, to see it contains no slander and is not potentially libelous. It is therefore advisable to allow at least a token sum for legal matters in the budget. Under the same argument, you may wish to write in a sum to cover your bookkeeping costs.

However bright you are, you may also need advice on the basic contract between you and the sponsor or TV company, even if there seem to be few complications. Although contracts are discussed in chapter 10, their complexity often requires you to take a lawyer to do a preliminary overview. For example, whether you do the contract yourself or use a lawyer, some commonsense points are worth keeping in mind before entering the contract.

- Check with whom you are dealing and research their reputation. This is of particular importance when dealing with distributors.
- Make sure you have a clear chain of title to all intellectual property.
- Make sure you understand the contract and the meaning of all conditions and terms like *net profit.*
- Try to limit your representations and promises. A television station will try to make you warrant or guarantee that your soul is pure. Try to add the phrase "to the best of my knowledge" if you can get away with it.

Lawyers are expensive, so it's worthwhile looking around for someone who specializes in documentary and who also doesn't charge a hand and a foot. Such people do exist. Shaun Miller in Melbourne, for example, has become doyen and adviser to dozens of documentary filmmakers because his advice is sound and he understands that filmmakers do not have the funds of high-tech millionaires. Make people like Miller your friends, because they will be an incredible help throughout your career.

Personnel

You are probably the producer and director of the film. Don't wait to see what's left in the kitty when the film is finished—budget a payment for your services from the start. Payments to the writer, director, and producer usually appear as lump sums, under the heading of "above the line costs," though the director may also be paid by the week. This is usually done in network contracts where the Director's Guild of American (DGA) specifies what at least the minimum payment should be per week.

What should the writer, director, and producer be paid? There is no fixed rule, though many people pay the writer about 5 percent of the overall budget and the director about 12 percent. I usually budget for the producer to be paid the same as the director. A lot depends on the bargaining position of the parties. If you want somebody special, then you have to be prepared to pay a premium for him or her. If the writer is a member of the Writers Guild (and you are working under a Guild contract), then you will have to pay at least union scale, and the same is true if the director is a member of the DGA. The situation becomes complicated if you want a DGA director, as you may have to sign a contract with the directors' union and also employ a DGA assistant.

Payment to the narrator is something else entirely and varies according to his or her fame or bargaining power. A half-hour narration might be as low as a few hundred dollars or as high as a few thousand. If you want the best or the most well known, then you have to pay accordingly. If you have a really prestigious public-service film, you may be able to get a "personality" to do your narration free or for a token sum donated to charity. Even so, it's best to write in a sum for narration.

General Overheads

Overheads can amount to a surprisingly high proportion of your costs. You must think about office rent, telephone bills, administrative help, transcripts, messengers, duplicating services, and any general help you will need. If you are shooting abroad, you must add not only general travel costs for the crew but also costs for medicines, a "handler," film dispatch, and customs clearance. Even if you bring the film back home by yourself, the customs authorities may require an agent to clear it with them. So that's another item on your list.

Station Overheads

I sometimes think the best job in the world is to run a PBS station. After the station gracefully agrees to give its backing and show your film, which will bring it a lot of prestige, and whose funds YOU have raised alone, the station may want to add an overhead of 21 per cent or more to the budget. This theoretically is for all the help and publicity it has given you, no matter that when you've used the station's non–air-conditioned editing rooms or an office, you've actually paid for them. Find out what you are getting for that 21 percent. It's an awfully big chunk of the budget, so see if you can lower it in negotiation.

Contingencies

However prudent you are with the budget, you may find that the film costs are running away from you. The usual problems are that you need more shooting days than you thought or that the editing goes on longer than you reckoned. But the problem can be something else entirely. A few decades ago, for instance, the Hunt brothers tried to corner the world's supplies of silver, and for a few months, the price of silver rose astronomically. As a direct result, film-stock prices also suddenly rose. This meant that contracts signed before the rise did not adequately cover the real price of stock. You want another example? A friend of mine did a film in 2006 that necessitated a massive amount of air and land travel. After contracts were signed, the price of fuel suddenly skyrocketed, with oil reaching $110 a barrel. You can imagine the effect on the budget. That's where the contingency in the budget planning came in to save him.

The contingency element in a budget shields you from the unexpected; it's a hedge against overruns. I usually budget about 7.5 percent of the total budget as contingency. This sometimes leads to arguments with sponsors who fail to see why a budget cannot be 100 percent accurate. In that case, I usually omit the contingency but specify in my contract a fixed number of shooting days and a fixed amount of stock. If more time or more stock is needed, then I get the sponsors to pay for these items.

Obviously, you have to use a certain amount of common sense and discretion in all this. It's no use arguing your rights, feeling your position is totally justified, and then losing the contract. This means that the contingency sometimes becomes mostly a matter for your own internal consideration: budget, and then add the 7.5 percent to see what a really comfortable budget should be. You then know both the preferred and the bare-bones cost for the film.

Profit Margins

The underlying message of this book is that you can and should be able to make a decent living from producing documentary films. Now comes the time to mention the word *profit*. Should you put in a figure for company profit, and if so, what should it be? The answer to the first question is definitely yes. But people, and sponsors in particular, have a funny attitude on this score. They reckon if you are the writer, director, or producer, then you should be satisfied for the amounts paid in these roles and should not ask for a company fee. This is nonsense and applies to no other business. If I run a garage, which is mine but registered in a company name, I expect to be paid as manager and for the company to make a profit. The same reasoning applies to filmmaking. You may spend half a year making a film and the other half writing scripts and proposals, chasing down other projects, and trying to get various ideas off the ground. Meanwhile, rent has to be paid, taxes accounted for, and electricity and telephone bills settled, you have to eat, and you have to entertain prospective clients. It is only the company profit written into your film that allows you to exist the other half of the year.

That answers the first part of the question more fully, but what should the profit margin be? This is hard to answer, but 12 to 15 percent is certainly within reason. However, that 15 percent is taken on the total budget without the contingency. Similarly, the contingency is taken on the original budget without the profit margin.

Invoice, Bills, and Receipts

When you run your own office, keeping order becomes the motto of the day. This is particularly true in regard to the tracking of the invoices you send out, the bills you receive, and the guarding of receipts. I repeat, receipts should be guarded with your life and kept in very good order. They provide a daily record of your expenses and are vital as proof when you come to do your income tax. And by receipts I mean everything, from the $5,000 purchase of a camera to the $30 for gas.

Budget Example

Up to now, I have tried to provide you with a broad view of what to expect and what to put in a film budget. However, in order to let you see how this all works in practice, below are one detailed budget and two outline budgets. The first was an estimate for a major-network film, *Peace Process*, with everything budgeted down to the last dollar. The second budget relates to the proposal I set out called *Gonna Travel On* and represents a much more modest budget, which is only outlined rather than detailed. The third budget represents an outline sketch for what might be involved in a simple, ten-minute public-relations film with few location or logistic problems and that could basically be filmed by just two people.

BUDGET FOR A ONE-HOUR VIDEO DOCUMENTARY, *PEACE PROCESS*

Production Budget for Shooting on BetaSP Video. Project Length: 8 months

Producer and Staff	Weeks	$ Rate	$ Total
Writer-Producer-Director	28	2,250	63,000
Associate Producer	22	1,000	22,000
Production Assistant	24	750	18,000
Researcher	8	700	5,600
Production Manager/Coordinator	7	1,200	8,400
PR Fringe: 12% of $78,900			9,468
SUBTOTAL			126,468

Preproduction Travel	Days	Persons	$ Cost	$ Total
Egypt		2	280	560
Jordan		2	150	300
Norway		2	930	1,860
USA (NY–Washington)		2	200	400
Eilat		2	160	320
Taxi and phone				400
Israel van and gas	5			750
Per Diem	16	2	50	1,600
Hotels	13	2	150	3,900
Extras				650
SUBTOTAL				10,740

Production Crew and Equipment (with Overtime)	Days	$ Cost	$ Total
Cameraperson and Beta SP Video	21	1,250	26,250
Soundperson and Equipment	21	300	6,300
Accessories			
Lights, Lenses, etc	21	150	3,150

Van rental and Gas	21	150	3,150
Per Diem Shoot (6 people)	7	50	2,100
Makeup Artist	6	200	1,200
Per Diem	6	50	300
Expendables			500
PR Fringe (USA): 16% of $3,450			552
Helicopter	(3 hours)	per hr/750	2,250
SUBTOTAL			45,752

Production Travel	Persons	Days	$ Cost	$ Total
Crew				
Norway	5		930	4,650
Egypt	5		280	1,400
Jordan	5		150	750
USA	5		200	1,000
Eilat	6		160	960
Per Diem with Hotel	5	12	200	12,000
Per Diem Eilat with Hotel	6	2	50	600
Extras				2,000
Excess Air Baggage				1,500
SUBTOTAL				24,860
In Israel				
Travel	5	7	50	1,750
Hotels	5	2	100	1,000
SUBTOTAL				2,750
Talent				
Norway				1,600
Egypt				350
Jordan				150
USA (NY–Washington)				200
Per Diems with Hotels				2,800
SUBTOTAL				5,100
PRODUCTION COST SUBTOTAL				78,462

Shooting Stock	Units	Days	Weeks	$ Cost	$ Total
BetaSP Tape					
(30 min.)	70			30	2,100
(1 hr.)	5			60	300
SUBTOTAL					2,400
Archive Material					
Rights USA (20 min. at $3,000 per min.)					60,000
Israel (10 min. at $1,000 per min.)					10,000
Library Viewing Days		15		100	1,500
Archive Researcher		15		175	2,625
Copying and Rights to Stills					1,000
Transfer Tapes (15)				60	900
Transfer Time (20 hr.)				60	1,200
PR Fringe: 16% of $2,625					420
SUBTOTAL					77,645
Editing Offline					
Editor			18	1,800	32,400
Assistant			10	800	8,000
Avid Rental and Space			18	2,100	37,800
Meals and Supplies				600	600
Transcripts					3,000
Narration, Recording, and Edit					800
Shoot stills					1,000
Dubs with time code					3,000
PR fringe: 16 percent of $30,000					4,848
SUBTOTAL					91,448
Editing Online					
Editing			3	1,750	5,250
Editor			3	500	1,500
Paintbox and animation (Chyron)					1,500
Sound editing effects					3,000
Sound mix (15 hours)				250	3,750
D 11 stock for master					500
Title sequence					2,000
Music, original or cues					3,000
SUBTOTAL					20,500

Office and Administration	Months		$ Cost	$ Total
Office				
Rent	7	1,200	8,400	
Computer and printer				2,800
Telephone, fax, mail		7	300	2,100
Copies, stationery supplies				800
Bookkeeper		6	500	3,000
Playback unit VHS and monitor				800
Messenger				500
VHS stock for dubs				300
Entertainment				600
Shipping				1,200
SUBTOTAL				20,500
Professional				
Legal				3,000
General-liability insurance				2,500
Production package insurance				2,500
Errors-and-omissions insurance				3,000
SUBTOTAL				11,000
Miscellaneous				
Research materials				1,000
Consultants			400	6,000
SUBTOTAL				7,000
Travel and lodging, producer and talent to and in United States				
Airfare producer (4 return flights, TA-JFK)			1,200	4,800
Airfare talent (4 return flights, TA-JFK)			2,500	10,000
Lodging producer (USA)		5	1,500	7,500
SUBTOTAL				22,300
TOTAL				**468,463**
Contingency (7.5 percent)				35,135
GRAND TOTAL				**503,598**

NOTE: Station overhead and publicity are not included.

Peace Process was made for a major PBS station and was a very complex film to bring off. It meant shooting in five different countries, and coordination was a nightmare. Luckily, I had a great production manager who was also a wizard with figures and in seeing we kept to the budget.

Gonna Travel On was a much-simpler, more modest film and far easier to budget. To get the film off the ground, I submitted the proposal to three foundations. Below is the outline budget, which I had to provide to all of them. It is nowhere as detailed as the *Peace Process* budget, but you can still see very clearly where all the money is going. The foundations required that you split expenses according to "below line" (basic production costs) and "above line" (key personnel like writer, producer, director). They also make no allowance for company profit.

OUTLINE BUDGET FOR FIFTY-TWO-MINUTE VIDEO *GONNA TRAVEL ON*

	Persons	Units	Days	$ Cost	$ Total
Crew					
Cameraperson			20	350	7,000
Assistant cameraperson			20	300	6,000
Soundperson			20	250	5,000
Production manager			15	250	3,750
SUBTOTAL					21,750
Film and sound equipment					
Camera			20	400	8,000
Sound equipment			20	125	2,500
SUBTOTAL					10,500
Stock					
Cassettes		60		20	1,200
Larger cassettes		8		30	240
SUBTOTAL					1,440
Foreign filming (Germany, United States)					
United States		1		1,200	1,200
Germany		3		800	2,400
SUBTOTAL					3,600
Travel and per diem					
Car and gas			20	150	3,000
Per diem		4	20	50	4,000

Hotel	2	7	13	1,820
SUBTOTAL				8,820

Editing

VHS transfers	30		20	600
Logging and viewing	30		20	600
Stenograms	10		20	200
Digitizing	35		20	700
Offline edit room		35	200	7,000
Offline editor		35	400	14,000
Online		3	400	1,200
Online editor		3	400	1,200
Narrator			1,000	1,000
Translations for editing			1,000	1,000
Preparing master BETA				1,750
Preparing master DVD				200
Music and film archives				5,000
Sound editing		3	800	2,400
Music				1,500
SUBTOTAL				38,350

Other expenses

Legal	1,000
Insurance	2,000
Office	4,000
Posters and advertising	2,000
SUBTOTAL	9,000

TOTAL BELOW-LINE EXPENSES	**93,460**

Above-line expenses	**$ Total**
Writer (5 percent)	4,673
Director (10 percent)	9,346
Producer (10 percent)	9,346
TOTAL ABOVE-LINE EXPENSES	**23,365**
Contingency (10 percent below-line cost)	9,346
GRAND TOTAL	**149,536**

The assumption in the budget for the film below is that this is a simple in-house video, which can be made with you and your partner carrying out all the main production tasks. Although you are shooting and editing yourselves and actually own the camera and editing equipment, these items should be added so that you can see the real costs of the film and the returns you are getting on the equipment each year.

OUTLINE BUDGET FOR TEN-MINUTE

PUBLIC-RELATIONS VIDEO *SUPER SUPER MARKET*

	Days	$ Cost	$ Total
Crew			
Cameraperson	5	250	1,250
Soundperson	5	150	750
Equipment			
Camera and sound	5	250	1,250
Cassettes and extras		500	500
Travel and per diem			
Van and gas	7	125	875
Food for two people			
(two days extra for research)	7	80	560
Editing			
Editor	10	250	2,500
Edit rooms and equipment	10	200	2,000
Extras and sound mix			1,500
Office, phones, insurance			
Sum allowed			750
Writer, director, producer			
Sum allowed			3,000
GRAND TOTAL			**14,935**

In this case, you would probably not break down the budget for your clients but merely tell them the film will cost $15,000, a very reasonable sum for a ten-minute film.

10. Financing Your Film

AFTER WRITING THE PROPOSAL, you face your key challenge: how to raise the money for your film. If you are doing a film that you can shoot and edit by yourself, and filming is confined to your local area, then you have few problems. Even with only a modest amount in your bank account, you can probably go ahead. But if the budget is somewhere, shall we say, between $30,000 and $300,000 and involves a lot of travel and use of archive materials, then you have some serious thinking in front of you.

As mentioned in chapter 5, a friend told Mark Harris the best solution for raising money was to marry a rich girl. But not all of us can do that or would want to do that. Another solution, as in the times of the Medicis, is to find a rich benefactor. When I interviewed Emile de Antonio for my book *The Documentary Conscience*, he told me this was exactly his strategy.

I have always been good at raising money. I have raised over one million dollars to make left-wing films. I don't come from a poor background, and I have always known people with money. Anyway, there was this nice liberal millionaire called Eliott Pratt, who gave his occupation as sharecropper. He was a liberal, very rich, and he hated McCarthy, and I went to see him. We met at his house and then went over to Seventy-third and Third where there is a place called Allen's.

We had a hamburger and a couple of drinks, and I told him what I wanted to do. [The film that eventually came out as *In the Year of the Pig*.] Eliott thought and then said, "Well how much money do you think that would cost?" I said, "I don't know. I have never made a film." So he said, "Well, what if I put up $100,000 to start?" I said,

"Wait, first I have to get a corporation established." Later the meal check was brought, and he tipped 20 cents and then did indeed give me the $100,000. In the end, the film cost a lot more.

Well, we should all be so lucky! But few of us have such generous friends and have to plan our fundraising strategy a little more carefully. Basically, there are five or six ways to raise money for a film, apart from a rich marriage, robbing a bank (well, maybe not after the latest economic crisis), and inheriting a fortune. They are via:

- Television companies
- Foundations, public and private
- The help of friends
- One's own resources
- Funding it with backers, and aiming at a commercial venture

Television Companies

When I first took up filming in England and wanted to raise funds, the television company or network was my first port of call. Although the BBC was closed to outsiders, doing virtually all its filming in-house, there were always Channel 4 and plenty of independent commercial stations around. And with luck you would get total funding. OK. It's now time to let out a big sigh! Times change and not necessarily for the better. Here is what John Marshall, the founder of Docos Communications, a very acute British critic, coproduction expert, and producer, has to say on TV and funding:

Television is dead, at least for financing serious documentaries. It will linger on for a time as a distribution system, making a small cash contribution but the days of fully funded, ideas-driven films are gone.

Television, especially public-service television, once saved the documentary genre by investing in projects, then serving them up to vast audiences. The penny-pinching days of Grierson chasing corporate sponsorship were superseded by a golden age of broadcasting money. Some documentary filmmakers even got rich, or at least earned enough to live comfortably. More important, they could plan their next film with some expectation that it might be made. Those were the '60s, '70s, and '80s.

No longer. The fragmentation of the television market means that few channels, with their falling audiences, can afford to contribute more than a fraction of a film's budget. At the same time, political pressure on public service broadcasters, especially in Europe, leaves them with fewer resources to back serious films that area minority taste.

I think John is overly pessimistic. A deeper look at American, British, and European broadcasting seems to indicate, to me at least, that all is not lost. In the United States, for example, funds are available from public broadcasting and a host of cable channels such as the Discovery Channel, National Geographic, HBO, A&E, History Channel, and a few others. The competition for money may be stiff, but money is available. For most documentary filmmakers, the first port of call is usually the Corporation for Public Broadcasting (CPB) and the Public Broadcasting System (PBS). In a note, specially written for this book, John Fox, Emmy-Award–winning producer of the 13/WNET series *Heritage: Civilization and the Jews* sets out how the system works.

CPB gets its money from the U.S. federal government, and its role is to pass the money on to the system as a whole without making editorial decisions. CPB was established to serve as a kind of "firewall" between the politics of Washington and the system so politicians and their allies could not micromanage the editorial decisions of public broadcasting programmers. CPB sometimes earmarks money for specific initiatives (currently *America at the Crossroads* and *New Voices*), and it accepts proposals from producers. A large percentage of CPB money flows to PBS for them to pass on, but some flows to other entities such as the Independent Television Service (ITVS).

PBS is an affiliation of public broadcasting member stations (rather like a UN for those stations). Member stations pay dues to PBS in return for a set of programming streams, and PBS uses the money from members as well as money from CPB to fund its operations. It also has a sizeable fund that it uses for programming. Individual stations as well as individual producers can approach PBS for money, and PBS programming officers judge the value of the projects and make individual grants to those they feel are sufficiently important.

PBS has occasionally acted as producer in its own right, mounting and launching series, though this has tended to be a source of strain between PBS and member stations that are also producers (in particular the large New York and Boston member stations).

PBS posts instructions on its Web site for producers interested in having their work considered for funding. Anyone interested can go to the "Producing for PBS: A How-to Manual for Producers" section of the PBS Web site for the manual with guidelines and instructions.

John Fox mentions ITVS above. It's a funding organization worthwhile examining in detail. ITVS was created to serve as a programming and funding source that would complement PBS by supporting programs that PBS was not likely to fund. Its mission statement declares that it wants to work with independent producers who take creative risks, advance issues, and represent particular points of view not usually seen on public or commercial television. In particular, they are committed to programs "that address the needs of the underserved and underrepresented audience," and among its signature series is *Independent Lens.* The monies awarded to different projects varies, but it is interesting that ITVS runs a special Diversity Development Fund that awards up to $15,000 to producers of color to develop single documentary programs.

Usually, American foundation grants are limited to American citizens. ITVS, however, is willing to award grants to foreign producers and has special instructions concerning the matter. ITVS grants come with one major condition, to which you must pay attention. If you are awarded production funds, you have to give ITVS exclusive U.S. TV broadcasting rights for seven years. Producers should access the ITVS Web site funding page for further information.

Another entity of interest which Fox thought worthy of mention is POV, or Point of View. POV has its own autonomous programming and production staff and is funded by CPB, PBS, various foundations, and PBS member stations. As its name suggests, POV covers documentaries that are highly controversial and might not get funded in any other way. Usually, POV supports twelve to sixteen films a year and is looking for films with a strong perspective and contemporary relevance. Thus, Marlon Riggs's opinionated in-your-face *Tongues Untied* found a place there, as did Ellen Bruno's *Satya.* If you are making your film with the help of a television station, that's fine—so long as you are the only one making decisions about editorial content. Here your best approach is to make enquiries straight to POV, which you can find by Googling "POV film funding."

Apart from the above suggestions, you can turn directly to your local PBS station for money for your film, and, occasionally, they'll come through for you. More often, they'll be willing to provide you with a letter of support and promise you an outlet when your film is made but leave the fund-raising up to you. Occasionally, however, they may be running their own particular documentary series, and if your film subject coincides with their interests and what they need, they might give you a more sympathetic ear. 13/WNET New York, for example, currently runs the documentary series *Wide Angle*, which deals with international affairs and subjects such as women's rights and human-rights abuses. If you are wild enough and impassioned enough to want to do a film on Darfur refugees or the situation in Myanmar, 13/WNET would be a possible station to apply to. Channel 13 also has a program called *Religion and Ethics*, which also occasionally takes independent programs.

Outside of New York, another interesting PBS station to turn to is WGBH, in Boston. WGBH is the originating station for *Front Line*, which is mainly about foreign affairs and world events. This means that one week you'll be looking at a documentary on the aftereffects of Hurricane Katrina and the next on the poisoning of a journalist critic of the Russian regime. WGBH also broadcasts *The American Experience*, which deals with major stories in America's past such as the lives of various presidents, or Ric Burns's study of the Donner party.

One of the gems in the crown of WGBH is *NOVA*, a science series that places great emphasis on look and stunning visuals. On average, the shows are budgeted between $400,000 and $600,000 and can vary from an investigation into the origins of swine flu to an update on the Dead Sea Scrolls. However, to get a sense of the competition, you should realize that *NOVA* only produces twenty shows out of the six hundred or so submissions it receives every year.

The non-PBS channels also offer some opportunities for documentary filmmakers, but here, too, the portals are quite competitive, at least as far getting financial support. Like *NOVA*, HBO also claims to have an open-submissions policy, but in practice, few make it through the front door. Under the guidance of Sheila Nevins, president of the documentary and family section of HBO, only a few miscellaneous projects are accepted each year, but their range can be very wide. Recent HBO documentaries range from *A Father . . . A Son*, about Kirk Douglas and Michael Douglas, to *China's Unnatural Disaster* to *Which Way Home* about the difficult journeys of Latin American child immigrants to the United States.

While National Geographic trundles on, and A&E offers some interesting openings with *Biography, American Justice,* and *Mysteries of the Bible,* the real phenomenon of the last two decades has been the growth of the Discovery Network and the opportunities offered by that expansion. Under its banner, it now includes Discovery: The Learning Channel, Animal Planet, and the Travel Channel, plus Discovery Kids, Discovery Wings, Discovery Health, and Discovery People. All offer opportunities for the independent filmmaker. The range of the network, which goes in for series as well as individual films, is very broad and sometimes makes one think that no subject is sacred. For example, while glancing through one week's *TV Guide,* I found the following Discovery films: *The Rise and Fall of the Mafia, The Secret World of Toys, The Secret World of Speed Demons,* and *Robots Rising.* As I said in an earlier chapter, you must know what is happening with the market. And remember, however bizarre the films seem to be, there is obviously a popular audience for them.

The Discovery Channel, like most networks, is very specific about the information it requires when making a submission. First, before doing anything, you must sign a release letter for the network, something many filmmakers object to doing. This letter absolves the network from any future claims that it stole or copied your ideas. I would, therefore, suggest that your film be well advanced and maybe well into preproduction before you submit it to Discovery, lessening the chances that your idea will be copied. Having signed your life away, you then submit a one- or two-page proposal that besides outlining your idea will include:

- The film format
- The production team and the job performed by each member
- Résumé with credits for each member of the team
- Demo tape
- Budget summary, showing how much you expect from the network
- List of coproduction partners
- Production timeline

The necessity of focusing your efforts continues when you go overseas and are trying to get help from the BBC or Channel 4 UK. Like the U.S. commercial networks, the BBC was closed to outsiders for years. Owing to the intervention and pressure of Margaret Thatcher's Conservative government, both the BBC and the English commercial channels have now opened their doors to independents—a policy pursued by Channel 4 since the start. Since the BBC produces more than two hundred hours of documentary features per year, there is much time to fill.

The BBC is actually divided into two main channels, BBC One and BBC Two, but BBC Two is the main producer of documentaries, which they hope will be "redemptive, inspiring, purposeful, and which push the boundaries." Sounds almost as if they are looking for student vicars. BBC Three, Four, and Five, all new digital stations, also carry documentaries. BBC TV Center is based in London. Like so many networks, the BBC runs an online submission process. Here the rule and approach are the same as elsewhere. Try to find some way to communicate with the commissioning editor personally before submitting. Otherwise, the likelihood is your proposal will remain unread. And this is where personal acquaintance at film markets and pitching sessions (discussed later in this chapter under "The Pitching Forum and Film Markets") becomes so important.

If your film can fit into a series or the broadcaster's documentary strands, you stand a better chance of having an idea accepted than if it stands alone. Try to find out what's going on. BBC strands have varied over the years and include:

- *One Life.* This is a forty-minute look at people in contemporary England, and a good example would be *Oldest Drivers in Britain.* The series advertizes that it is interested in alcoholism and bullying, Alzheimer's disease, and anything that's not been told before. So it gives a wide canvas.
- *Storyville.* The BBC flagship international documentary strand has stories varying from one on the problems of Roman Polanski before the U.S. courts, to the state of the Bollywood film industry. Recent films include *Children of the Chinese Circus* and *Hammer and Tickle,* about the history of Russian communism through the national jokes.
- *Omnibus* and *Arena.* For their part, these series deal with music and the arts.
- *Time Watch* and *Ancient Voices.* Topics cover history, the first modern, and the second ancient.
- *Horizon.* This, together with *Tomorrow's World,* is the British equivalent of *NOVA.*
- *Bookends.* Here the subject is literature and literary profiles, such as portraits of Frank McCourt, Robert Cheever, or Elmore Leonard.

The recent main strands on Channel 4 include:

- *First Cut.* This series is devoted to the work of up-and-coming directors.
- *Cutting Edge.* These are films that are supposed to reflect contemporary Britain and the modern world. Recently screened examples include *Killer in a Small Town*, *Eight Minutes to Disaster*, and *Would You Save a Stranger?* Obviously, the films weren't made for the British tourist association.
- *Secret History.* This features history.
- *State of the Nation.* Looking at Britain's public services is this series focus.
- *To the Ends of the Earth.* Travel and adventure are explored.
- *The Family.* This is an observational series about a family.

Channel Four also broadcasts a number of one-off documentaries. Before writing this chapter, I looked at their current offerings, which included *Marriage Techniques for Beginners* and *Queen Victoria's Men.* The first was not a sleazy how-to but a newly married man's diary of his first steps in uncharted territory. The second film, based on diaries and memoirs, was about the men, handsome and otherwise, who surrounded Queen Victoria in her early years as queen.

Both networks can be reached online. What makes things a trifle easier at the BBC is that it issues *The Foreign Producer's Guide*, an invaluable pamphlet with all the ins and outs of working for the BBC and the lowdown on current series. It can be obtained by going into the BBC Web site or writing to the BBC at its Wood Lane office in West London. I also advise you to look at *Video Age International*, which, from time to time, publishes details of television programming, not just in England but around the world.

Finally, a word on European stations that take documentary broadcasting seriously. The key ones that might interest you are ARTE, which works out of France, and ZDF and ARD, which are public stations working out of Germany. What is useful to know is that in the past, all three stations have been very open to foreign submissions, particularly ARTE, which likes to call itself Europe's prime cultural channel. That's nice to hear when so often *culture* is used as a dirty word. But with all three stations, the thing to remember is that they are European. That means they need something that will touch their local audiences, such as films on Hitler's women or on Mussolini's love life. If you are thinking of doing a film on soil-conservation problems in Nebraska or on an aging senator from Milwaukee, I wouldn't send it to ARTE. However, something on Hollywood scandals or great racing drivers of the world could well get accepted.

The Coproduction Market

Even if you manage to raise funds from a television station or a network, you may find the sums they have allocated to you are insufficient to cover the budget. You are left with only partial funding. This is especially true if you are involved in a major production. You've raised enough money to give you hope, but where do you go from there? One answer is applying to foundations and private donors. The other is to consider the possibility of a coproduction with your own company and a number of diverse international television entities. This was the model used for the financing of the series *Vietnam: A Television History*, a coproduction among WGBH of Boston, Central Independent TV in the United Kingdom, and Antenne-2 of France. *Vietnam* was a huge thirteen-part series, with the contribution of WGBH itself being supported by various foundations. However, coproductions more often relate to one-off films, and this is where opportunity arises.

The usual approach is to try to interest one or two potential partners in different countries and then let the interest of one pique the curiosity of the second or third party. Let's imagine you want to do a film on Hemingway and American painters in Europe in the twenties and thirties. You then decide to broaden this idea into two films on ex-patriots. PBS is interested in the idea, as is 13/WNET New York, which agrees to serve as the U.S. presenting station. The funds they can give you are limited, but 13/WNET agrees to give you a strong letter of support. You then apply to various European networks such as NDR or CanalPlus and attach the letter of 13/WNET. One of the networks responds positively, and you take things from there. John Marshall, who declares above that TV documentary financing is dead, saw and sees coproduction as one possible answer to financing problems.

A first response to the gathering storm started in Europe in the 1990s, when the European Union's Media Program backed a number of initiatives that created the international documentary co-production market. Various broadcasters from different countries—the UK's BBC, Germany's ZDF, Denmark's TV2, France 2, ARTE, to name but a few—agreed to co-finance significant independent films in return for broadcast licenses in their own territories. Other rights, and revenues, remained with the filmmakers. The result was that while financing became more complicated and international, it remained possible. Most crucially this was forward financing through pre-sales, which meant a film's budget could be fully funded before starting production. Expensive and elusive gap finance was unnecessary. Producers stopped mortgaging their houses.

The Foundation Scene

As I've hinted throughout this book, if you want to do a film on sexy and popular subjects such as searching for sunken submarines, hunting for Nazi war criminals, or about Hollywood idols who've had a sex change and now run exclusive brothels, you will probably have little trouble raising your budget. But if your subject is not sensational, does not give the Discovery channel an orgasm but makes a quiet appeal to the human mind and intelligence, and assumes that most people have an IQ higher than fifty, things are harder. The answer, parallel to applying to the television stations, is to beat a path to the doors of public and private foundations, corporations, and private donors.

Most independent filmmakers I know who work seriously in documentaries raise their funds through applications to local arts councils and foundations. These foundations have, in fact, become the chief sources of independent-film financing in the past decade. Broadly speaking, these agencies are divided into federal, state, city, and private funding bodies. Generally, government agencies tend to fund research and preproduction, while private organizations are more inclined to give completion monies. Sometimes, you will go back to the same source more than once, the first time to cover research and development, the second time for production.

The big hitters among the granting bodies are the Rockefeller, Ford, MacArthur, and Guggenheim foundations; the American Film Institute; the New York Council for the Arts; the National Endowment for the Arts (NEA); the National Endowment for the Humanities (NEH); and the Sundance Documentary Fund. Funding is intensely competitive, and dozens of applicants are turned down for every grant awarded.

Application forms, once all the necessary information is filled in, can also run longer than the Bible.

Also note that most state humanities commissions work hand in hand with the NEH. Similarly, most state or city arts councils work closely with the NEA. In addition to the above, you should be aware of the existence of the Independent Documentary Fund, which is run by CPB.

While the big foundations are open to submissions on almost any subject, most smaller foundations and family foundations tend to limit their grants to their own specific areas of interest. The Soros Foundation states its interests as being the support of open societies, education, and social justice. In a sense, this is an advantage, as you can limit your hunt to the foundations whose interests coincide with yours. A little bit of hunting on the Internet can pay off in enormous dividends.

Let's say you want to do a film dealing with Christian faith. A little bit of Internet research reveals the possibility of support from the Broadcasting and Film Commission of the National Council of Churches and/ or the International Society for Excellence in Christian Film and Television. If your film has wider faith issues, you might turn to the Fund for Unitarian Universalism. If your subject touches on Jewish or Israeli matters, then you should be applying to the Jewish Chautauqua Society or the Lynn and Jules Kroll Fund for Jewish Documentary Film, which provides finishing funds.

On humanitarian and ecology issues, consider applying to the Horizon Foundation, Zellerbach Family Foundation, Hugh M. Hefner, or the Foundation for Grass Roots Organizing. Where did I find these names? By five minutes' research on the Internet, which also gave me the names of films these organizations supported.

And so you proceed, always looking for the support group whose interest match your own. Melinda Levin's interest in farming issues led her straight to the Dixon Water Foundation and to the Quivira Coalition. Why Quivira? Because its mission statement states that it wants "to build resilience by fostering ecological, economic, and social health in western landscapes." Bingo! This is exactly what the film is about.

Maybe your interest is in gay rights or lesbian issues. Start Googling, and you'll find not only are you not alone but hundreds of organizations share your concerns and goals. So you could apply to the Ahmanson Foundation, American Express Foundation, AT&T Foundation, and Ferris Foundation in Boston. The Web sites can easily be found through a search.

The list of foundations and their interests is endless: ecological, gay, Christian, social justice, education, health, human rights . . . all have their supporters whose purpose is to give away money that will help their mission's goals.

Many rich groups have also established small family foundations. Usually, they don't go in for much publicity, and you find out about them from word of mouth or by noting their names as funders when you've viewed someone else's film. Sometimes, you can find out about them by asking around. You see in your local newspaper that a millionaire in your community keeps expressing his interest in helping Afghan refugees in America. Maybe he's just the guy who can help you with your film, and a short note to him won't go amiss. And maybe, just maybe, you have some rich generous friends interested in your work. Don't be bashful. Talk to them. Who knows? Maybe the one or two thousand dollars they put into the kitty will make the final difference.

One thing you should remember, with reference to family foundations or the help of friends, you must make all the funds transferable to you via a nonprofit foundation. You can set up a nonprofit foundation yourself, though I prefer to work through an existing agency as an intermediary. When funds are channeled through a recognized nonprofit organization, the donor becomes eligible for various tax concessions on the donation. The effect, for example, is that though the donor gives you, shall we say $1,000, he is allowed a proportion of that as a tax offset, his $1,000 donation really puts him $500 or $600 out of pocket.

For its part, the nonprofit foundation will probably take 5 percent of the donation as its administrative fee and pass the rest on to you. Working this way, via a nonprofit intermediary, you get $950, the intermediary gets $50, and the donor gets tax help. So everyone is happy!

The Funding Proposal

Though I covered proposal writing in chapters 7 and 8, it is worthwhile adding a few words on the specific shading needed for foundation requirements. Most foundations require a proposal that clearly states the nature of the film, its objectives and limits, and a well-defined distribution-and-use program relating to the film. Foundations, at least the bigger ones, also like to play it safe by requiring the participation of "experts" to provide academic respectability to a project. Such requirements sometimes make sense, but they are obstructions to the filmmaker operating in a field that doesn't require scholarly penetration. What you have to do is acknowledge the basically conservative nature of big-foundation activities. The art film, the science film, and the educational history film pose few challenges to them. In contrast, the political, investigative, or critical film rarely finds a place in foundation funding without a great deal of trouble.

The result is that this setup may favor those who can write good grants over those who are poor grant writers but better filmmakers. This has actually long been acknowledged, so many of the major arts foundations will go out of their way to offer you help in writing and framing your grant application. Various periodicals can also help you considerably in this grant-writing business, such as the *AFI Education Newsletter*, the *Independent, Foundation News,* and the journal of the Independent Documentary Association. A number of good books have come out recently that can guide you through the grant-writing maze. Among the best of these are *Shaking the Money Tree* by Morrie Warshawski, *Money for Film and Video Artists* by Douglas Oxenhorn, and *Get the Money and Shoot* by Bruce Jackson.

Most good libraries have a copy of the foundation list put out by the Council of Foundations. This gives you the name and addresses of the major foundations in the United States, together with a list of projects that they support. A few days perusing that list (it is immense) can be worth quite a few dollars in your pocket.

Unlike the national endowments, many small foundations will simply ask you to send them a short letter describing your project. Later, they may ask for additional details, but in many cases, your short letter of about two pages *is the application.* Five things go into it: tell them who you are, what you want to do, why there is a need for your project, the amount of money you are seeking, and why they should support you.

Your letter to business corporations should also include:

- A list of established corporate sponsors
- Your background
- A request for an appointment

Don't be surprised if your letters to small corporations fail to elicit a response. That's because you and your project don't interest the would-be sponsor, so why should he or she waste time and money in replying? However, even if you get the slightest nibble, it should be pursued.

It is imperative that your proposal be well organized. Often the funding agency has a specific application format. If not, then try including these sections in this order:

- Abstract and/or summary
- Rationale for making the film
- Description of the film
- Personnel and grant-overseeing agencies
- Distribution ideas
- Budget needed
- Appendixes with letters of support
- Your connection to a nonprofit foundation (for tax deductions)

Raising the Funds: Some Examples

In my early years as a filmmaker, I mostly worked for well-endowed TV stations or made PR films for various hospitals, education agencies, and welfare organizations. The advantage in working this way was that the films came completely funded. The last twenty years, I've been working as an independent. A few times, the funding road has been easy (though never strewn with roses), but more often, it has been quite difficult, with half of my time being allocated to raising money and half to actually making the film.

In order for you to understand more fully what happens in fundraising, I thought I'd share with you the rocky-path process mentioned above, which I followed on my last two films, *Stalin's Last Purge* and *Waves of Freedom*.

The idea for *Stalin's Last Purge* came to me after reading *Koba the Dread* by Martin Amis and *The Great Terror* by Robert Conquest. Both books outlined the awful years of oppression, suffering, and death in the USSR under Joseph Stalin's dictator regime. As a Jewish director, however, I was very much drawn to the fate of the Jews under Stalin in the years 1941 to 1953. This was an astonishing period, when his policies underwent breathtaking changes from courtship of the Jews during World War II to their murder and annihilation in the last years of his life.

Three stories in particular lodged in my mind. The first concerned the fate of Solomon Mikhoels, the great Yiddish theater director, who headed up the Jewish Anti-Fascist committee during the war but was brutally murdered by Stalin's thugs in January 1948. The second story dealt with the secret trial and subsequent execution of fifteen Jewish writers, poets, and intellectuals in 1952 in Moscow's dreaded Lubyanka prison. Lastly, I fixed on the story of the Doctors Plot. Stalin invented a plot wherein Jewish doctors were supposed to be scheming to poison various members of the Kremlin including Stalin. Publication of this fictitious plot, early in 1953, was supposed to lead to a public trial and execution of the doctors and possibly forced exile of thousands of Jews from the big cities to Siberia and Kazakhstan. The plan never happened as Stalin died in Mach 1953, and shortly afterwards, the new regime announced that the plot was total fiction.

So here were three very sad, but also very good stories that I thought I could lace together into an interesting hour film. Over the course of a few months, I read everything I could about Stalin and the USSR from 1917 to 1953. I also started hunting for living witnesses to these events and managed to trace the sons and daughters of most of the principal characters in my film, such as the daughters of Mikhoels. On the basis of all this information, I wrote a ten-page proposal and gave my intended film the title *Stalin's Last Purge*.

As I live in Jerusalem, my first step for funding was to send the proposal to the documentary department of Israel television and to three Israeli film foundations. When I phoned up the head of the television documentary department, he told me, "Alan, I've got ninety proposals on my shelf. Eventually I'll get round to yours." He never did. Meanwhile, two of the Israeli foundations turned me down, saying they weren't in historical docs. Fair enough. The third foundation, however, gave me $5,000 for film development. Not much but enough to get me on my way.

Using some of the development funds, I went to New York to investigate TV interest and a few foundations. The documentary program director of 13/WNET liked the project. He thought it might work for a new series they were trying to set up called *States of Terror* or something like that. Alas, the series never got off the ground. OK. On to the foundations. One in particular interested me, the Charles H. Revson Foundation. I'd met the foundation's president years before, and although he'd consistently turned down my films, he always finished up by saying maybe the next one. And here I struck gold. It turned out that the foundation had recently funded the translation from Russian into English of the protocols of the secret trials of the Jewish writers and intellectuals. My film was proof of the value of that work, and the foundation gave me a very substantial sum to start filming.

While still in New York, I went to see a multimillionaire whose film biography I had done some years before. During that filming, he had told me he was passionately interested in all questions to do with Stalin and his murderous policies. "Something should be done to publicize those murders," he had told me. Recalling those words, I went to see him in his luxurious Forty-second-Street office and pitched my proposal. After an hour, I walked out of there with a nice check and left him a promise to list him as executive director.

One of the biggest problems of the film was that it required massive amounts of still and archive materials. In my reckoning, these items were budgeted at $50,000. In the end, I went to see one stills archive that, believing in the film, very generously allowed me to use the stills for nothing. The National Archives also provided me with a lot of material, merely for the cost of duplication. Finally, there was the question of using Russian archives. A friend gave me advice: "Don't approach the archives yourself, because as a foreigner, they'll charge you the earth." I took that advice and saved a bundle. In the end, I found archive costs were only about $10,000, as against the $50,000 I'd budgeted.

Even so, I was still in the red but at least had enough to do some serious editing. After three months, I went back to the Revson Foundation and showed its president and key adviser a rough cut. They loved it and gave another small grant. So I was almost home. Finishing funds eventually came from the Foundation for Jewish Culture documentary fund. This was my second application to them, as they had already turned me down once.

After six months' break, I was ready to start a new film *Waves of Freedom*, about American volunteers who, against the will of the British, brought displaced people (DPs) to Palestine in 1947. I had to raise the budget in a slightly different way, and the Revson Foundation couldn't help me, as it had stopped funding films. In the end, *Waves* was done as a coproduction with Germany and France.

Once again, I applied to all the usual Israeli film foundations and got turned down. Israel TV showed some enthusiasm but was going through a budgetary crisis, so no help there. This time, it took four good friends to get me going. Each gave me a donation of about $3,000, which was run through a nonprofit foundation. So that was $12,000 in the kitty for starters. I tried selling the film idea at a pitching session in Sitges, near Barcelona, having made a three-minute trailer to go with the presentation. (See more on pitching later.) Four stations were interested, and after months of negotiations, ARTE and ZDF agreed to come in as coproducers. I then made a slightly longer video (eight minutes), rewrote the proposal, and started sending the package around to friends and strangers in England and the United States. Another $20,000 was raised this way. Finally, one of the heroes of my film introduced me to two American millionaires, who came up with the finishing monies. Again, somehow, the monies had been raised.

Experience and reputation help in fund-raising, but even then, it can be quite a sweat. Take the example of Leslie Woodhead. Leslie is one of the greats of English broadcasting, having very successfully run Granada (Manchester, England) TV's docudrama division for years. Ten years or so ago, he decided to take the path of the independent producer . . . but one who had dozens of contacts the industry. Even so, it took Leslie quite a while to raise the coproduction budget for his film *How the Beatles Rocked the Kremlin*, which describes the effect of the Beatles and their music on culture and change in the then-existent Soviet Union. Leslie writes:

> It took two years for me to raise the funding for the Beatles film. First the BBC signed on and commissioned the film, but as it was for *Storyville* on BBC 4 that provided only around a third of the budget. Then ARTE joined in, having been recruited at the Amsterdam Forum pitching session (IDFA). Just a year ago, 13/WNET in New York came through with $100,000, which meant that eighteen months after I started, I had a budget to complete the film. I persuaded the City of Liverpool to provide ten thousand pounds with funds from the City of Culture 2008 budget—invaluable in helping to fund the vital archive material.

An Australian friend of mine, Monique Schwartz, told me a while ago she had an idea for a documentary she wanted to call *MamaDrama*. The idea of the film was to show how the Jewish mother had been portrayed on the screen, and possibly the stage, from the 1920s until today. I thought it was a great idea but that it would be very difficult to raise money for the film. Happily, I was wrong. Melbourne-based Monique eventually raised the production funds from multiple international sources that included SBS, Film Victoria, and the Film Finance Corporation (all Australian); NOGA Communications (Israel); AURO (the Netherlands); ARTE (France); and ZDF (Germany).

As always, luck has a great deal to do with things. You always hope it's going to be there. At the moment of writing, I am trying to raise co-production money for my docudrama *Condemned to the Penal Colony*, whose proposal I set out earlier. So I am in negotiations with the drama department of ARTE, have found some development money in Tasmania, and will shortly submit the proposal to ABC Australia, the BBC, and HBO. I'll also make a submission to ITVS, under its foreign-producer section. Will anything come of all this? I have to believe so.

The Pitching Forum and Film Markets

These days, most submissions to commissioning editors or for foundation grants are made online. That means you are anonymous, lost in the crowd, and have no human or personal contact with the recipient of the e-mail. You don't know whether he or she even reads your letter or promptly hits the delete button. One recent trend helps you slightly in avoiding that situation. That trend is the growing enthusiasm for and expansion of documentary pitching and selling markets. Markets like MIPCOM (in Cannes), NATPE, Leipzig, and MIP-TV have now become essential venues for pitching opportunities, making sales, schmoozing, meeting people, and exchanging ideas regarding single films and series, financing and coproducing.

You are probably familiar with the pitch or the fast sell from films such as Robert Altman's *The Player*. Here, merely seconds after the film has begun, we are provided with a classic demonstration of the Hollywood pitch when a young, eager scriptwriter tries to sell his idea in thirty seconds flat to a bored movie mogul. Well, before you laugh, you should know that the pitch has invaded the documentary scene with some notable success. Many documentary markets and festivals—such as Hot Docs in Toronto, IDFA in Amsterdam, Medimed in Sitges, Spain, and Sunnyside in La Rochelle—offer the opportunity to pitch or discuss your film proposal with various commissioning film editors with a view to getting it financed.

A film market such as Medimed, in Sitges near Barcelona, sends out an open call for film proposals. The submitted proposals, besides setting out the film idea, also have to include budget, producer's background, details of funds already raised, and the names of any television stations already involved in the project. Later, the proposals are vetted by various judges, and from the two hundred proposals submitted, maybe thirty are selected for the market. That may seem to you like a seven-to-one chance, but if your proposal is any good, it will probably get through.

At the market itself, you then have fifteen minutes to sell your idea before a general audience of, say, sixty people and a motley collection of twelve or so commissioning editors, who may come from the United States, Britain, France, Italy, Belgium, and Germany. None of the people present will have read your long proposal, which was merely a means to get you into the market. However, they will have before them a short précis of your film and its budget.

The candidate pitchers normally follow one another at fifteen-minute intervals. This means that you might have eight pitches in the morning and another eight pitches in the afternoon. In practice, the fifteen minutes at your disposal is split into two sections. First, you have seven minutes to talk about your film and show any visual materials you have prepared. The other eight minutes are left for questions and reactions by the commissioning editors. It helps to have a friend take down the names of the few people who've shown a particular interest during your pitch.

Pitching to such an audience may seem a frightening, off-putting process, but provided you are prepared, it really isn't. Also, in order to help novices at this procedure, many markets also provide a training session with an expert to help you get the best out of your presentation pitch. As you have very little time at your disposal, you have to hit the right bells from the word *go*. You have to explain briefly the length of the film, its story and dramatic importance, how much money you are seeking, and for whom the film is intended. Thus, if it is a film of only local interest to New Yorkers, don't expect German or French television to be interested. But if you can link your film to the audiences of those present, you are one step ahead.

What is also vital is to explain what special materials you have, what, if any, special access to the subject you have, and why the subject is magical and will captivate audiences everywhere. For a few minutes, you have to stand up straight, look people in the eyes, show tremendous confidence, and become actor and fairground barker. Recently, in Spain, I pitched a film about a hunt for the lost treasures of the Jewish Second Temple. These treasures included the mysterious Ark of the Covenant and the fabled golden Candelabra that Titus took to Rome. Right at the beginning I said, "This film is essentially *Indiana Jones* meets *The Da Vinci Code*." And at the end, "And if I find the treasures, I'm going to give up filmmaking and live in luxury in Rio de Janeiro." Low humor, yes, but the jokes reinforced the pitch.

If you are lucky, four or five people in the audience will respond favorably to your pitch. Your job is then to try to spend a little bit more time with them at the market, get their names if you haven't already, and follow up by sending the full proposal and pressing your case through e-mail and phone calls. To be realistic, only one or two of the five will turn out to be truly interested. But if they can supply $10,000 or $15,000 toward your film, you are well ahead of the game.

Pitching sessions are useful for another thing besides selling your own film. They are a fair barometer of what the TV market wants or seems to be interested in. This was shown to me at the first pitching session I ever attended, in Brisbane, Australia. Fifteen people pitched, and everything was presented from proposals about the alcoholic problems of Aboriginals, through crime in New Zealand suburbs, to saving Balkan children from becoming pregnant. In attendance were commissioning officers from Discovery, National Geographic, Arte, the BBC, and many other exalted stations. Most of them, however, seemed bored out of their skulls by the presentations and gave the impression (false, I hope) that they had only come to Australia to escape with their mistresses to the Queensland rain forests.

Then a young man, Dave, made a presentation that made them all sit up and come awake. As far as I can recall, he wanted to make a film in which he followed in the footsteps of his grandfather. When his grandfather Jake was a young man, he had gone down the river Nile on a canoe. He had subsequently been chased by natives, missed being speared, and had swum to a desert island while being pursued by sharks. While on the desert island, he had discovered a secret cave guarded by a mysterious cult. They, too, had tried to kill him, but he stole a boat and fled to another island with their precious green idol. On this second island, he was hailed as a god and given the natives' fairest virgin as a bride. And so on and so on. I've forgotten all the details, and maybe I'm making some up, but you get the gist of the story. "And," said Dave, opening his arms with a wide gesture to embrace all the audience, "I want to go exactly where Jake went and see what has changed since his day."

The commissioning editors went mad. "Absolutely right for Discovery." "No, in the BBC we pay more." "What do you mean. There is only one rightful home for this film, and it's National Geographic." And so it went on, till Dave left trailing clouds of glory and hunting for a pen with which to sign the television agreements. Meanwhile, the rest of the filmmakers were left to pick up the pieces. Believe me, it was a very salutary lesson in what sells and what doesn't.

Tomorrow's Financing

For some final thoughts, I asked John Marshall, whom I quoted earlier and who has tremendous experience in financing, to summarize for me where he thought we heading in the next ten years. I also asked him to consider the position of documentaries made deliberately for profit. My two main questions to him were very simple. Can serious documentary films be financed in what he sees as a post–television age? And if so, how?

> Yes, they can. But the model has to be rethought, and producers will have to learn new skills. The documentary genre is also likely to change accordingly.
>
> The first point is that producers are now completely on their own. There is no gospel, and the priests have departed. They can look at alternative models to see if they fit, but, at base, it's a time for them to become as creative as they ever have.
>
> Some, like Michael Moore and Morgan Spurlock, use the commercial theatrical model. They put themselves in the frame and make "documentary" as entertainment, using the methods of feature-film financing. Cinemas and DVDs are the primary means of distribution. They may make lots of money. They may not make anything. Bu the aim is to maximize revenues, just like commercial feature films.
>
> Others will try crowd financing, where many "supporters" invest small amounts in issue-based films they believe in, like End of the Line and The Age of Stupid. The Internet makes this easier, and the subjects can range from environmental issues to anticapitalist critiques. Not much of a range, but with this sort of financing, the investors are the audience. This approach is likely to merge with funding from private foundations and wealthy angels. DVD is the primary distribution system, with some theatrical release to build publicity and reviews. Internet dissemination, especially of small clips, can play a role. Television has a problem with many of these films because of their political positioning.
>
> NGOs are a potential source of public-diplomacy financing that many are eyeing, hoping to combine it with television money or crowd

financing. It works like this: most NGOs—the UN agencies, international aid organizations, and some national government bodies—operate huge audiovisual budgets aimed at advancing their goals through public diplomacy—propaganda and education as it used to be called. Traditionally, much of this money was wasted in producing naïve, low-grade material for distribution to the converted. Why not invest instead in high-end, television-ready documentaries that make serious points about your work and objectives and may reach audiences you could otherwise never hope to influence?

Each of the alternative funding models is likely to influence the film's content, approach, or aesthetic. The theatrical model can encourage documentary as entertainment. Crowd financing can evoke the exposition of the party line. Public-diplomacy funding can result in the equally humorless presentation of an NGO's good works. In short, all may lack the degree of reflexivity and self-knowledge that many regard as the mark of an outstanding film.

There is a fourth alternative: public equity investment. This accepts there is a market failure with regard to documentary financing and requires a fundamental belief that documentaries can make money or at least enough to cover their costs. Essentially, it requires public investment or development and production funding up-front, probably to a limit of about 50 percent, on the basis of pro rata pari passu. The public investor hopes to recoup from revenues and sales and to make a profit, which then goes into a revolving fund for future investments.

The remainder of the budget—real market money—needs to be found from wherever possible: broadcasters, primarily, but also perhaps DVD or theatrical advances, tax credit, or private investment. The one aim is to get a promising film to market, where it can make revenues to repay investors.

What is different is that while such investment is likely to come from public agencies, it is only concerned with a commercial return, not with cultural or other objectives. It addresses market failure, not an agenda of cultural or political development. Within wide parameters, any content or aesthetic is acceptable if it will make money.

A number of public European and UK film agencies have started to experiment with the model—not least, Screen East with *Making a Killing* and *Shed Your Tears and Walk Away*—and so far the results are promising. On the basis of existing deals, both films will recoup their budgets and go into profit.

What it clear, however, is that public equity investment requires a skilled executive producer to represent investors' interests as against those of the production company, much as commissioning editors did in the glory days of television. This is a new model with which some producers will feel uncomfortable, especially if they are used to tapping loosely administered "cultural" funds. The difference is that the market-focused public-investment model offers real and serious production money. This means a chance for all concerned to make a decent return and the creation of permanent, revolving documentary production funds.

11. Production Contracts and Other Agreements

AS AN AMATEUR, a student, or occasional filmmaker, you probably entered in the past into a number of agreements or commitments. Generally, you tried to fulfill them but didn't always succeed. In your documentary class, you proposed film "A" as your end-of-term project and then turned in something totally different. You got yelled at by your professor, but there were no serious consequences. OK. Maybe you got a "C" instead of a "B." No big deal! As a part-time filmmaker, you did a small film for a friend's father about his garage-and-repair business for classic cars. You promised the film for January but delivered in April, and no one seemed to mind.

Now you are entering a new world. As an independent producer, running a serious film business, you will be entering into a number of agreements that absolutely have to be kept. If you break them, not only will your name and reputation suffer but also very serious financial consequences may follow. The aim of this chapter is to guide you through the most serious of the film agreements you are likely to encounter, give a few tips to help you to understand what you are getting into, and show you ways to avoid major problems.

The major agreements you may have to consider include the following:

- The production contract
- Option agreements
- Distribution agreements
- Agreements with participants, crew, and lawyers
- Bank loans
- Releases and permissions

Other types of agreements may come your way from time to time, but if you can handle the above, you will be in good shape.

The Production Contract

Preliminaries and Warnings

You've done a realistic budget breakdown, and your proposal has been accepted by the station or the network, or the hospital, or the university, or the like. In the case of the first two, they've probably sent you a letter saying, "We view your project with favor. It seems ideal for our *Secret History*, and we'd like you to telephone us for an appointment to come in and see us next week." In the case of bodies like a hospital or university, more or less the same procedure will be followed. You've got an informal agreement to go ahead, which is very nice, but now you have to tie it all up in some legally binding document. Until that agreement has been signed and dated by both sides, all you have are smiles but no commitment. That's a point very worthwhile remembering before you go out and buy your Bentley with the anticipated proceeds of your film.

Before you meet with your film sponsors or talk to them via e-mail, it is worthwhile taking a few minutes to think through your position and consider various things. For instance, in some cases, you may have been told in advance, say by the hospital, how much they are willing to pay for a half-hour film. More often, the sponsor, who may not have seen the budget, will want to know how much *you* are asking for your work. There will be timetable discussions. Do you know when you can start, and how long the film will take you? Have you thought about the film ownership or DVD distribution? Your proposal may have been very broad. Do you now know in reality how you are going to bring the film off? You are going to be asked a lot of questions as to what you want and your method of work, and the answers will form the basis of the terms of the contract.

Even though you've thought through the major terms of the agreement, many terms, conditions, and obligations will appear in the contract that you *haven't* thought about or considered. Although I discuss many of the these in my analysis below, there is one rule you must follow: *Read all the small print*. Even what seems to you a minor sentence may involve you in major obligations.

When you go into these precontract meetings, be prepared to argue for what you want. You are still in negotiations. This is where you put some of your cards on the table. You state what you want, and you see if you can get it. As my mother would say, "If you don't ask, you don't get." Or as the sages put it, "If I am not for myself, who is for me?" Obviously, a certain discretion and tact are needed at this stage. You don't want to be overly greedy and blow the deal, neither do you want to be timid and have oppressive terms forced on you. So you play it cool and carefully.

Let me give you one example of "if you don't ask, you don't get." A few years ago, I pitched a film somewhere in Europe, which was taken up by one of the country's bigger TV stations. I was overjoyed. Then I asked about money. After a week or so of humming and hawing and "That's not our concern, that's dealt with by department X," they came through with what I thought at first was a nice sum. I was still starry eyed at having the film idea accepted. On closer examination, I realized that the suggested sum wouldn't take us very far. I phoned a friend who worked for the network. His advice: "They've got plenty of money. Ask for more." This I did with great trepidation, and department X suggested a sum a quarter larger than the initial one. That was nice but still seemed to me on the low side. I phoned the executive producer who'd been assigned to me but whom I'd never met. I told him I needed a lot more money to make the film and asked what they usually paid for documentaries like mine. He named a sum considerably larger than what I had been quoted.

Armed with this information, I went back to department X and, like Oliver Twist, asked for more. Oliver was thrown out of the workhouse for his insolence. For my part, I was in a total funk that my chutzpa, or cheek, could lose me the total film. I was in luck. That didn't happen, and for the second time, they increased the sum. OK, I'd had a little inside advice, but the principle is still solid. There is no harm, after reviewing the total situation and the position of the sponsor, in asking for what you really need.

One thing you *don't* do is go ahead and do serious work on the film till you have the contract or at least a short, signed memorandum of agreement between the two sides setting out at least the basic lines of the agreement. Fail to follow that procedure, and you'll be in for a lot of trouble, as I know from my own bitter experience. The story is as follows.

About five years ago, a producer friend of mine, let's call him George, asked me to write and direct two one-hour films for him about German war criminals. We verbally agreed a good sum for my work, and as I'd worked with George many times, that was fine. The films involved an enormous amount of research and a lot of work on script planning. My starting point was to write a proposal, plunge into German records, and read masses of books on the period. For his part, George started trying to find finance and eventually netted some big promises from a German TV station . . . let's call it XYZ, to back the films. He also brought in some money from a Dutch TV station.

For a while, we were riding high. Then the German station XYZ asked to see draft scripts for the two films. No problem. I turned them in, each script being about eighty pages long (I put everything in first draft and then drastically reduce). The Germans then made comments and asked to see a second, then a third draft. George and I were then invited to Berlin, at our own expense, to discuss the films further. They also asked for a fourth draft. We spent an amicable day and a half together in Berlin, and I received the German comments for a fifth draft. Two months later, the German commissioning editor and his assistant came to our offices in Jerusalem to push matters further ahead. They saw my latest scripts, viewed a mass of archives we had collected, and heard our shooting plans. George wined and dined them, and at the end of a week, the Germans were massively satisfied.

On the last night, we raised glasses, and the German promises were made. "Yes, my friends, your very good health. Signed agreement in three weeks, and first-stage payment [about $20,000] in a month." For a few weeks, we corresponded. Everyone seemed to be happy. Then, out of the blue, "Sorry. We are not going ahead with the film." No follow-up explanation. All the massive work was for nothing. No contracts had been signed. We'd been working in good faith, but it was all one-sided. There was nothing we could do but swallow a very bitter pill. Lesson? You don't start working till you have a signed agreement. There is a PS. The films were eventually made, being basically self-financed by George, who put his company into vast debt for a number of years to do it.

You may be dealing with the production contract before scripting or after scripting. The situation I mentioned above, where I did a preliminary draft, is not unusual. The mistake was taking it further than that.

The usual procedure is for the sponsor, after preliminary discussions, to send you a draft contract for consideration and comment. Sometimes, you may be the one preparing the contract, but that doesn't happened very often, at least not in broadcasting circles. The contract may run to three pages or thirty, but in reality, there are only a few major points to consider, with all the rest being elaboration. I have set out below the main elements of most production contracts and have tried to bring to your attention some of the points that you should consider in detail.

Definition of Length and Purpose

The contract will generally define in its first few paragraphs the kind of film you are doing, its object and purpose, its maximum length, and the medium and gauge in which it is being shot. It may read, "*Hear Me, Brother* is a one-hour, 16 mm, color film on the treatment of deafness for use in specialist schools for the deaf," or it may say, "*Shoot First, Questions Later* is an hour videotape on youth gangs in the slums of Caracas." These first few paragraphs will also set out the parties to the contract. After giving your address and name, you may be defined throughout the contract as "the Producer," while the broadcaster may be defined as "the Station." Alternatively, you may be defined as "the Licensor" and the station as "the Licensee." Later, the rights and obligations of both parties will be set out at length in the body of the contract. These preliminary first few paragraphs may also be surrounded by *whereas* and *wherefore*, but that's just legal jargon you don't have to worry about.

Time and Manner of Delivery

The sponsor will try to get you to commit to a specific delivery date. You have to be careful because of the immense number of things that can go wrong and cause you to miss the deadline. For example, you may not have gotten your full funding for a coproduction, in which case it would be folly to commit to a problematic deadline. I prefer, if possible, to put in a definition of intent rather than commitment: "The filmmaker will endeavor to deliver the film by such and such a date," or "The filmmaker understands that the film is due for presentation on July 15, 2011." Avoid being penalized for late delivery. This is important, since even with the best intentions in the world, there may still be delays. Normally, the sponsor understands why the film is delayed and is sympathetic but not always. So watch out. Sometimes, the sponsor may want the film for a specific broadcast date. In that case, you have no option but to sign your life away.

The contract will also specify what has to be delivered and in what way. This covers prints and other materials. I usually try to press for delivery of one print (if it's a film) with any others to be paid for by the sponsor. With videos, you can afford to be a bit more generous. I also ask the sponsor to pay for the combined reversal internegative (CRI, used in making multiple film prints).

If you are doing a videotape, the sponsor will probably require a number of BETA masters and DVDs. You should also double-check whether copies have to be delivered in any foreign formats, such as PAL or SE-CAM, if you are working in the United States.

Sometimes, when you are doing a PR film, you may be asked to deliver a great number of DVDs. Make sure you are covered for the cover design of the DVDs and the cost of making the distribution DVDs.

You should also make sure you read very carefully the technical requirements for delivery when you are working with a broadcaster. Do they want the film in HDTV? Do they want it in 4/3 ratio or 9/16? And are you following all their sound, titling, and subtitling standards? Often, the broadcaster will issue a booklet or small cassette containing delivery instructions. Make sure you read it.

While working on my film *Waves of Freedom*, I noticed a small phrase in the draft contract about delivery, which I missed first time around. It said that all the materials should be of the highest and most immaculate quality. However, I knew my film would contain a lot of archive footage, which would possibly be scratched or out of focus. I brought up this point with the other side and said because of that I couldn't possibly sign the contract as drafted. The contract was subsequently amended in my favor to take note of that point.

In some contracts, the sponsor or station asks for all the rushes, original tapes, negatives, and sound material to be handed over at the conclusion of the film. This is fine in most cases of PR films, but if you have materials that you think may be valuable in the future, try to hang on to the negative or original tapes. In a broadcast film, where you've maintained ownership (see later on this), you hold on to all the materials.

Personal Responsibility

Some contracts may demand that certain people do specific jobs; this usually concerns the writer and director. This happens when you've sold the film on the special abilities of those two or when the film is the special baby of either the writer or director. However, you should allow yourself an escape hatch in case of unforeseeable factors such as illness.

Film Cost and Payment Schedule

The agreement should state clearly both the overall sum that the sponsors will pay for the film and the times of payment. In most cases, payment will be made in stages, and you should try to ensure that these payments come at convenient times. You need money *before* shooting to pay for stock, possibly hire equipment, and pay for crew. You don't want to be paying for these items out of your own pocket. A typical payment schedule on a $100,000 film might look like this:

1. $10,000 on signing contract
2. $10,000 on script approval
3. $30,000 on commencement of shooting
4. $20,000 when shooting is completed and editing starts
5. $10,000 on approval of fine cut
6. $10,000 on completion of mix
7. $10,000 on delivery of print

Sometimes, the number of stages is reduced to only three or four, which might be (1) signing contract, (2) commencing shooting, (3) approval of rough cut, and (4) delivery.

All this seems fine regarding payment, but you should also note that reality can sometime look quite different. Though you fulfill all *your* commitments in time, the other party might be much more dilatory. So don't be surprised if payments don't arrive in time or that it takes several phone calls and letters to get stage payments. That's the way the game is played. I did a film for France for which a big-stage payment was due after approval of the rough cut. The money only arrived after the film was finished. Unfortunately, in most cases, there is not much you can do, as usually you need the big station more than it needs you. So you grin and bear it.

Two other money points to look out for when working with a foreign company on a coproduction are trying to ensure that the deal is done in the currency most favorable to you and being aware that some of the payment may be held back because of foreign tax regulations. You can usually recover that foreign tax withholding if you can prove you pay tax at home, and it may be a matter to discuss with your accountant.

One vital matter is to get the contract signed and some money paid before stage-two script approval. Unless you do this, the sponsor can hold you over a barrel with its approval. They can ask for more and more script changes before you have even signed a contract. This means in practice that you are doing a tremendous amount of work without any formal guarantee or agreement, and the tension will drive you crazy. Earlier, if you remember, I described the disastrous consequences of all this when we dealt with Germans. A good rule is first the signature, then the work.

As I suggested before, there is, of course, a definite rationale behind the timing of the payments: you should have all the necessary money at hand when you need it. Your big first costs are going to be research, shooting, and editing so you need money in advance to cover these stages, especially shooting. You also need money for your own salary and living expenses; I like to receive about 20 percent by the time the script is approved.

One common bugbear is the sponsor who procrastinates on approvals. This can happen on approval of the rough cut, fine cut, or the final narration. It is also surprising how often the person who can give the approval seems to be ill or away on vacation. Thus, unless you are careful, you can find yourself in an exasperating situation, waiting weeks for payments while the sponsor plays around with small changes or recovers from vacation sunburn. One way around this is to put in specific dates as well as film benchmarks for payment. You could specify $10,000 payment on approval of the fine cut or on February 5, whichever comes earlier. The sponsor may or may not agree with this point, but it's worth battling for.

Can you ask for extra payments besides the principal sum? No. The contract usually stipulates a total fee for delivery of the film, and once that sum is on paper, that's it—thus the importance, as I've stressed before, of very accurate budgeting.

If I am doubtful about the number of shooting days or if the sponsor argues for the inclusion of something that I'm not sure about, I try to put in a clause covering additional payments. The clause might read, "The licensee [the television station] will pay for any additional days' shooting at the rate of $1,000 per day and will also pay for any film stock used on that day at cost." I am not fond of this additional clause, and neither is the sponsor. But sometimes, it may be the only way to safeguard your neck and your pocket.

Generally, you have to watch out carefully to see if the sponsor wants you to employ all sorts of cute video and CGI effects. They may turn out to be horrendously expensive, and you want to be sure your contractual sum covers this. If you think the sponsor may suddenly dump on you the need for high-cost special effects when you are nearing the end of the film, then protect yourself with an item regarding extra payments.

Approvals

The contract should stipulate someone who can act as the sponsor's agent and give approval at various stages of the film. When you are working with a broadcaster, the approval is usually given by the executive producer of the show. Whatever the situation, try to make sure that the approval has to be given by someone who understands the film and whose judgment you value. In most PR films, the person giving the approval is the person, usually the vice president in charge of publicity, with whom you've been dealing since the first discussion of the film. But this isn't always the case. Sometimes, the sponsor decides that some other top executive, such as the president of the university, has to give approval. From then on, it's all a matter of luck. Get someone who is intelligent and sympathetic and understands a little about film, and you're home free. Get the opposite—and it happens—and you're in trouble. Above all, try to avoid approval by a committee. That's the road to disaster. Remember the old adage, "A camel is a horse designed by a committee." So keep your fingers crossed, or, better still, try to insist that the person giving approval is someone you know and trust.

Ownership and Territories

The best position is for you to own the film. You need to establish from the start what rights you have in the film, and ultimate ownership is best. In the long run, you are going to make much more money owning the film. This is because you can get extra payments for further distribution, and there is also the question of owning all the valuable ancillary rights besides broadcasting. The flip side of the coin is that the television station that finances you will also try to ensure that it owns the film because it's more money for them.

If you are the ultimate owner and are working with a commissioning TV station, the contract should state

- The licensing period given to the TV station
- The number of broadcasts allowed in that period
- The geographical area covered by those broadcast rights
- The situation regarding ancillary rights

Broadcasters are hungry and greedy. As I write, I'm looking at a draft agreement on my desk with a European broadcaster who asked for an unlimited number of broadcasts, over an unlimited time, for the total world . . . or as they put it, for the entire universe. I didn't sign the agreement, because I thought it was excessive and outrageous.

A more reasonable, and actually more widely used set of conditions, might be as follows.

- Licensing period—three years from first broadcast
- Number of broadcasts allowed—five, within three years
- Territories exclusively allotted to broadcaster—Germany, France, Austria, Switzerland
- Except for some limited digital rights, all ancillary rights to belong to the licensor (i.e., you)

In the above, you've actually made a great agreement for yourself. To begin with, you have the total right to license the film throughout the world except in the restricted territories. And even then, the named territories are only restricted for three years. Secondly, you've managed to keep all the ancillary rights. That means the rights for all DVD sales, rentals, educational sales, and the like are held by you. Those rights can be worth a lot of money, so you try to hold on to them.

Sometimes, a broadcaster will be willing to limit the years and number of broadcasts as above but will want to participate in any profits arising from further distribution or use of the film. Here, you have to estimate how strong your bargaining position is. If the broadcaster gave you the major coproduction finance for your film, then its demand for 50 percent of subsequent profits might be seen as reasonable. If it only gave you 10 per cent of the budget but wants 50 percent of the profits, obviously the demand is unreasonable, and I wouldn't accept it.

Warranties and Obligations

The broadcaster likes to make sure it is protected from every side, thus, it demands a series of guarantees from you, usually called *warranties*. This is just another word for obligations you have committed yourself to.

These warranties usually deal with matters such as ownership, copyright, and harm. You have to swear that all the materials in the film belong to you, and you have a right to use them. The penalties for a making a mistake on this go from torture, drawing, quartering, and hanging . . . OK, just kidding . . . to withdrawal from the contract and penal fines.

The issue of copyright features very strongly here, and you have to guarantee you have the right to use all copyright materials. You are to a certain extent covered by the existence of E and O insurance (mentioned earlier) if you have taken that out. Libel is also another subject the broadcaster wants to guard against, and even though the station may have its own surveillance lawyer, it wants you to guarantee the film contains no slanderous or libelous materials. On all these matters, breach of ownership, copyright, and libel, the station will hold you possibly liable for any actions brought against itself. As usual, it's a one-way system. If the station goes bankrupt or financially bottoms up after you start making the film, you usually get no compensation.

Credits and Changes

The contract with the broadcaster may define or repeat how credits have been assigned. That's fair enough. What you have to look out for is anything that hints that the assignment of credits can be changed at the broadcaster's discretion. This clause isn't usually used but if inserted can be dangerous. It can mean that although you produced and directed the film, for all sorts of reasons your name can been reassigned to a place of no importance. Imagination? No, because it's happened to me, and it hurt.

Another clause to be aware of is one that says the broadcaster can change or cut the film at its discretion *without consulting you*. This phrase is usually inserted so that the broadcaster can trim the film to its own broadcast requirements or leave space for commercials. For example, you may have made a fifty-two-minute film, but the broadcaster's air time is only forty-eight minutes. In that situation, you have to bend with the wind. But the situation can be trickier where you've made a fifty-two-minute film, and the station wants to cut it to forty-two minutes. The answer may be to insist that any cuts over four minutes have to be approved by you.

Miscellaneous Contract Clauses

The above paragraphs cover the most important points in the production agreement, but there is no limit to the things people will dream up to put into a contract. So what else can arise?

Contracts are drawn up by lawyers, who try to protect their clients from every catastrophe, real or imagined. Their answer is to put in the necessary, the unnecessary, and then some. There may be a discussion of publicity. You may be asked to take stills. You may be requested to abstain from immoral conduct that will bring the station into disrepute. You may be asked not to hold yourself out as agent of the sponsor. You may be told that though the film is being made and edited in the United States, it may be governed by English law. You may be told that all notices to the sponsor or broadcaster have to be written in red ink and hand-delivered to their office before ten o'clock in the morning.

I have already stressed the points that are vital for you, the filmmaker. As for anything else the lawyers write into the contract, look it over carefully, and try not to laugh at the more nonsensical points. Then use common sense. If you feel that an obligation is unfair, reject it. You may have to explain your objection at some length, but don't accept the clause just because someone has written it in.

Remember one thing. At this point, the sponsors want you to make the film as much as you do, so don't be afraid of arguing controversial points with them and looking after your own position. If you don't, no one else will.

Finally, if a lot of money is involved and you feel uneasy about your obligations or uncertain as to what you are really committing to, get yourself a lawyer—not one who merely deals with real estate but someone who understands something about the entertainment business. It's costly, but the advice will probably pay for itself in the end.

Option Agreements

What happens fairly often is that you read or hear of a book or read an article in a magazine and think, "Hey, that would make a great film," or "There's a good film idea buried in that article." This has happened to me twice over the last ten years. The first time was when I read a book about wreckers. The reference is to the groups who used to live around the seacoasts of England and by using decoy lights and beacons, lured ships on to the most dangerous and savage rocks in the vicinity. The wreckers would then go down later and plunder the wreckage, taking away money, goods, liquor, or whatever the ship was carrying. I could see the bones of a good film story there but knew I'd have to get the author's permission to use the book as a basis for the film. In other words, I could not start thinking about a production until I had procured the film rights.

The second time was when I saw an article in a magazine about a pilot who stole planes from under the nose of the British in order to fight a secret war. The article also referred to a book about the pilot. Again, a great idea for a film. I missed out on the film about the wreckers because someone had secured the film rights before me. With the pilot's story, I was more lucky and optioned the rights. So what is an option, and when do you use it?

A *film option* is an agreement to secure your right to possibly buy the film rights on an agreed-upon subject within a limited period in the future. The operative word is *possibly.* You see a book like the one on the wreckers. You'd love to make a film on the subject, but the rights belong to someone else, usually the author, possibly the publisher. You approach the author's agent. Yes, the film rights are open for purchase, but the agent wants $10,000 for them. You haven't got the money for an outright purchase, so you decide to take an option.

An option is a device to buy you time while you try to raise the money for the film. Basically, you agree to put down a small amount now, which ensures you the option to purchase the actual film rights at some specific time in the future. During the period of the option, all third parties are excluded from purchasing the film rights. Here is an example of the way the system works.

- You are interested in the book *The Unknown Pilot,* but it costs $5,000 to purchase the rights.
- The agent agrees, however, to let you have a two-year exclusive option for $500.
- At the time of taking out the option, you also agree on a price, $5,000, for the film rights if you decide to go ahead.

This now means you have two years to raise your film financing. If you succeed in raising the money within that time, you can then buy the rights for $5,000. You'll be paying $4,500, as the option fee is taken as an advance. If you can't raise the money in that time, then you forfeit the $500 paid, as that's nonrefundable, and then third parties can themselves bid for the rights.

In practice, you usually make the option renewable for a specific sum, say an additional $500. So say you've paid $500 for a two-year option but don't raise your money in that time; you then pay another $500 and are allowed another two years of grace.

What you also do at the time of the option is fix the terms of the actual rights agreement itself. The rights agreement, let's call it "the RA," is then attached to the option agreement as an appendix or supplement. If you are lucky, raise all the necessary money, and want to exercise your option after two years, the rights agreement itself is already there just waiting to be signed.

This means that right from the beginning of discussions on the option, you also have to think through very carefully the terms of the RA. Eventually, do you want to purchase just the film rights or also TV rights, DVD rights, educational rights, and so on? You may also have to consider whether the original author should get any percentage of any profit you make as producer. In a hypothetical example, if you made $100,000 profit on your final film (What a dream! What a dream!!), you may want to give the author 2 per cent of that. Or you may not.

One last word on options. The price you may have to pay for an option obviously varies with the fame and status of the parties. Nothing is fixed. If you are optioning a book from a relatively unknown author whose work has not been widely or particularly well reviewed, you will probably pay a low sum for the option and get it to extend for three years or so. But if you want to take an option on a nonfiction best seller, then expect to pay the moon.

The Distribution Agreement

Some people distribute their film themselves. Others take a professional distributor. In the next chapter, I discuss the pros and cons of each choice. However, if you do take a distributor, he or she will require you to sign a formal agreement with him or her. If so, you need to be aware of what terms and arrangements are likely to come up in the contract.

The main clause pushing the whole deal is your grant to the distributor of the right to license or sublicense certain rights in regard to the film. These rights usually include, but are not limited to, the following. The right to broadcast the film via:

- Free TV
- Satellite TV
- Cable TV
- Subscription TV
- Closed-circuit TV
- Or any other form of transmission known or to be invented

Hidden within all these phrases will probably also be the right to broadcast the film on pay TV, on ships, on planes, in hotels, and at army bases. In other words, the distributor wants to be able to get the film out anywhere and everywhere. And he or she will also want the right to do it via disk, tape, cassette, cartridge, or other media. The distributor will also ask for the right to sell the film as a DVD or license it for educational use.

Exclusive Rights and Territory

So far, you are with the distributor every step of the way. But what if he or she wants *exclusive* distribution rights, which is the usual demand? Here, you need to pause and think a while. What if you think there is a certain area where you think you can do a better job than he or she can? For example, you have done a film about a Christian community in a certain state and think you can promote the film better than the distributor among that community and definitely sell more DVDs to the community than the distributor can. If so, maybe here you share the rights or try to maintain some limited rights for yourself.

The question of *territory* also arises. The distributor usually not only likes to be exclusive but also wants world rights . . . or, as they put it these days, rights throughout the *universe*. But you may not want this. You may think that an English or French distributor will do a better job in England and France than an American. Maybe yes, maybe not. That's for you to investigate and judge. But the point is the distributor will, for starters, ask for exclusive distribution throughout the world and will be very unhappy if you don't grant that.

If you go ahead with giving exclusive distribution, you must, however, inform the distributor what areas are already taken. If you have been working with a European network such as ZDF, you will already have agreed that they have distribution rights in Germany, France, Austria, and Switzerland. Again, if ITVS has backed your film, that organization will have been given the broadcast rights for the United States.

In these cases, you provide your distributor with a copy of all the agreements you have with other broadcasters. Not only does this clarify the scene for the distributor but also allows him or her to see whether the broadcaster has taken up nonbroadcast rights or ancillary rights as well and, if so, for how long.

The distributor will also ask for a number of other rights, which we need not go into now. They involve things such as the right to translate the film, modify it slightly for foreign broadcast needs, put in its own logo, and the like. They are of minor importance to you. Where you have to pay real attention, however, is in all discussion of payments and gross fees.

Calculating Net Receipts

The aim of the distributor is to earn you a lot of money through his or her efforts but also to make some money for himself or herself in the process. How that is done is defined in the contract. Distributors make money by taking for themselves a percentage of the money received from licensing the film and other means and passing the remainder on to you. It all looks easy but can be a slightly baffling and tricky process. Don't be surprised if at the end of the day, you receive less than you bargained for.

You want to see why? Let's start at the beginning. Let's say you make a bargain with the distributor that he or she gets 40 per cent of the licensing fees, and you get 60 percent. Looks good. Maybe you can go even better and arrange that the distributor only gets 30 percent of the fees (oh, do I love that word *only*), and you get 70 percent. Then small deceptive words start appearing in the contract such as *gross* and *net*, and that's where you begin to get into trouble. That's because what you get, and what the distributor gets, are calculated in different ways.

Assuming a 60 percent, 40 percent share out, as suggested above, this is how the money division actually works on receipts of $1,000.

- First, the distributor takes his or her 40 percent cut from the total, or what's called *gross* $1,000 fees. This cut is called the *distribution fee*. At this stage, the distributor has $400.
- Next, the distributor will take a second amount called *direct distribution costs*, which I'll explain to you in a minute, and they might amount to as much as $250.
- Finally, you get what remains, which is called *net producer receipts*, and amounts to $350.

The deceptive item or items, which you never really paid attention to, are *the direct distribution costs*. These are expenses that the distributor runs up, but which according to tradition, he or she expects you to pay for in the end. They can include advertising, costs of attending film markets, foreign-language dubbing, audition materials, making show cassettes for showing to TV stations, duplicating scripts, and a catch-all phrase "all other distribution costs for which television program distributors are customarily reimbursed." Theoretically, "all other distribution costs" are all costs that contribute to the sale of the film. Maybe they do. But now I know why distributors smoke cigars, and directors just chew gum. OK, maybe I am being unfair. The reality is that in the end, a good distributor, and I say good, not mediocre, will probably make you more money than if you distributed the film yourself. Though that may be changing, as I discuss in the next chapter.

Deliverable Materials

The final important section of the contract appears under the head of deliverable materials. These are the materials that you will have to supply to the distributor so that he or she can begin to publicize the film and get it out to interested parties. Since the distributor will be supplying the film in many different ways, he or she has to have the materials at hand in order to supply all needs. For example, he or she will need not just an NTSC Digi Beta master but also a PAL Digi Beta. The distributor will also want the music and effects sound tracks, any promotional materials, credit lists, and copyright-registration documents.

All these you will probably have to hand over. However, the one item that is vital and many people forget to make is a music cue list. This is a sheet that shows the title and composer of the music, how much of the music is used in the film, whether it's original or purchased, and, if the latter, proof that all fees have been paid. The distributor may also ask for an errors-and-omissions certificate, but since this is so expensive, you can usually leave that aside till a broadcaster, usually American, insists on having it before screening the film.

Agreements with Participants, Crew, Lawyers, and All the Rest

While agreements on production and distribution are usually written out as long, formal, legal documents, agreements with your film participants, crew, and your lawyer tend to be much less formal. Sometimes they may be merely verbal agreements, sometimes they may take the form of a short, written note of your major agreements terms, usually called a *memorandum of agreement*. But whether verbal or written out as a few brief sentences, these agreements are serious, affect your film, and, according to the circumstances, can be legally binding.

Agreements with Participants

The usual practice is not to make any payment for someone who is interviewed in your film. This is not written in stone, and sometime you may, in fact, pay for the interview. I have done this where I very much wanted an expert's comment. The situation is different, however, when the participant is playing a dominant role in your film, for example, when you are following one particular family over a period of time. In Allan King's famous *A Married Couple*, Billy and Antoinette were paid for the director's two months' filming of them. Payment is also made in docudramas to secure the rights to reenact someone's life.

In these cases, a short agreement is usual made, defining how much the participants will get and the amount of access given to the director. Sometimes, the sides may settle on a fixed sum. Occasionally, the participants may want a share of any of the producer's profits.

Where problems often arise and should be settled when the deal is made is regarding the amount of say or censorship the participants should have over the final film. My own rule is "consultancy, yes . . . power to change editing, no." It sounds easy, but it is tricky. In Craig Gilbert's series *An American Family*, Pat Loud gave Gilbert permission to edit as he saw fit. She saw the editing and made little comment, as far as we can tell from reports. When the film came out, however, she objected to how she was portrayed, but having agreed to the director's terms, there was little she could do. Had Gilbert given Loud a veto on the editing, the film would have come out very differently.

Agreements with Crew

You settle your terms with the crew when you initially decide to employ them. You agree a daily rate or a weekly rate and then add any frills if necessary, such as overtime and travel. You also tell them when and how they'll be paid. Usually, this is all very informal, and all you need to do is make a note.

However, if you are working with someone for the first time, he or she may ask for something more formal. When I employed a new editor on an hour's film, she wanted me to write out how many editing sessions she would work and for what rate. All of which was fine.

Sometimes, the situation is reversed, for instance, when someone wants to employ you as a director or writer. If the employer is a major station, then the station will issue you a formal contract. You should think through what you want very carefully before signing on the dotted line. You may be coming from another city to work for the station. If so, you can ask for lodgings and transport. You can also ask for a basic food or per-diem allowance. The station may not agree, but then they might. No harm in trying. I would also try to enter the contract as an *independent contractor* rather than become a temporary employee of the station. The reason is that as an independent contractor, you usually get paid gross and then deal with income-tax matters yourself. As an employee, your tax is deducted automatically at source. Usually, the former situation works out better for you financially.

Agreements with Your Lawyer

Often when your head is reeling with the amount of agreements thrown at you, you go to a lawyer. You want him or her to look over the agreements and tell you everything is *kosher*, or fine. It is a practice I heartily approve of. But that advice itself costs money, and when lawyers can charge $300 to $400 an hour, you have to tread a little warily.

Normally, in a community of filmmakers, friends will be able to recommend a lawyer who is good, knows the film business, is interested in filmmakers, and also doesn't charge the earth. Such a person was recommended to me when I was filming in Australia. A friend told me of a young lawyer who'd become a guru and friend to the documentary community, loved filming, and gave his advice for a very low sum when he believed in the film. There aren't too many angels like this around, but they are worth hunting for.

You probably won't enter into a formal agreement with the lawyer, but you must get a rough idea of what he or she charges for work. You may also make some kind of a retainer deal with them, where they give you advice over a fixed period for a fixed amount.

Permissions and Releases

Both permissions and releases are forms of agreement frequently met with in documentary filming and worthwhile mentioning briefly.

Permissions usually come in two forms: permission to use materials and permission to work in some place or location. Permission to use materials usually concerns the use of stills, archives, or literary material necessary for your film, and I've discussed this matter at length in the chapter 9 on budgets. A contract will be necessary with the copyright holder, and you can't go ahead without that being signed.

Permission to work in some place is some thing else entirely. You may want to film in a home, in an office, in a workplace, in a public place, or in a museum or theater. In order to film in a home or an office, usually a verbal agreement is enough. In al the other places mentioned, you may need to get the agreement in writing. If so, make sure as far as possible that your permission is flexible regarding date and time of shooting. Sometimes, you arrange to shoot on Monday but then have a delay and can't shoot till Tuesday. If so, and you haven't made the permission flexible, it's tremendously frustrating to find yourself confronted by some petty official who takes pleasure in wielding power and stands by the letter of the law that you only have permission for Monday.

You should also consider the *personal release form* under the heading of permissions. This is a piece of paper signed by a film participant allowing you to use the footage in which he or she appears. Normally, you orally ask permission to shoot and then get the signed, written release when shooting is completed. Some directors also ask for the participant to give permission on camera.

Such a release is usually a matter of safety rather than necessity. Few states or countries have rules about privacy, and filming someone on the street is not a basis for legal action. If such a person wants to take you to court, he or she must prove harm. That's normally quite difficult, so why does one bother with a release? For safety's sake!

The release stops someone you have filmed from making trouble for you at the most inopportune moment. You have filmed a woman talking frankly about her boss. A week before broadcast, she gets frightened and goes to court to stop the broadcast, claiming she's been harmed and never gave permission. Showing the court the release form stops any threat of an injunction against the film.

Some people insist you should pay a dollar for the release to make it legal. I don't hold with that argument. The dollar is necessary as consideration if your whole aim is to make a contract. But what you are really doing by paying a dollar is getting proof of an agreement, which is different. My own feelings are that offering money leads to more complications than it solves, and I have never done it.

If you are doing a commissioned film for a television station, it will most likely provide you with its own standard release form. When I am doing a film on my own , my general rule is to keep the release as simply worded as possible; for example, "This is to confirm that I, Jane Wilson, have given Finchley Films Inc. permission for the interview filmed with me today to be used in a film called *Desert Ladies*, directed by Joe Smith, for showing on television and other outlets." My rationale for the simplicity is that there is no standard release form (and that's why I haven't provided you various examples), and the more details you put on the form, the more problems you raise in the mind of the signee. In many years of practice, I have had few problems with this simplified system. If you are hungry for something more complex and full, a moment's search on the Web under "film release forms" will provide you with dozens of other release-form possibilities.

12. Making Money

YOU'VE SWEATED YOUR GUTS OUT. Your film is finished. It's taken you six months, a year, two years to make . . . but who's counting? There it is, and you're actually quite proud of it. It's artistic. It's entertaining. And here and there it's quite moving and occasionally quite funny. Now you want two things. . . . or two main things. You want to get it out to as broad an audience as possible, and you want the checks to start rolling in. You don't want to become a millionaire, but it would be nice if the film made some money.

So now we come to the crux . . . how do you maximize the financial possibilities of the film, and how do you ensure the greatest distribution potential? How do you make your film connect with the widest possible audience? These are difficult and challenging questions to answer because the whole scene has gone through such radical changes in the last few years.

Basically, you make money from your films in four ways. Two of these have to deal with films that belong to others, and two relate to films that basically belong to you. First, you can make money by being paid for your services. Second, by what I'll call *contract residuals*. Third, you can employ a professional distributor to market your film. Finally, you can self-distribute, which is becoming an increasingly popular option. Let's look at these possibilities, one by one.

Working for Third Parties

Payment for Services

We've already mentioned the possibility of your being employed as a director or writer for hire. If you are working for a major cable station or a PBS station, you should, with luck, have arranged a good deal for yourself. A reasonable salary for a director in this kind of situation would be at least $400 to $500 a day. If you are working on a major hour documentary and are employed for twenty weeks, you can come away, before tax, with something like $45,000. If the film is also being made under director's guild rules and has a long life span, then you should also make some money from residuals. *Residuals* are the small amounts of fees paid to members of the director's, writer's, or actor's guild every time the film is rebroadcast after a certain amount of showings. If you are working as a writer, and the film is covered by the writer's guild rules, then you could come away with $16,000 or more.

This isn't bad money and will buy you quite a few cups of coffee at Starbucks. In fact, there is only one problem. Your work ends, and that's the end of payment. And it doesn't matter how well the film does, you don't participate in any future profits. This is the biggest complaint I've heard from friends of mine who are, or who have been, major directors and have worked for major networks over the years. Here and there, a few of them have seen the light and have set up their own companies in order to maintain an equity in the film.

Contract Residues

When your company makes a PR film or any other contracted film, you will have drawn up a budget as recommended earlier and put in a goodly sum for yourself as producer and director and, maybe, writer. You may even, as I suggested earlier, have put in a sum for company profit. You know from the start roughly what amount you're going to make on the film.

However, as it's your production, you are also considering the whole time how to save on expenses without detriment to the quality of the production. For instance, you manage to shoot in nine days instead of ten or edit in seven weeks instead of eight. These savings go to your profit at the end of the day.

If we compare *payment for services* with *contract residue*, you can easily see why the second is often the better deal. I'll give you a personal example.

In the midnineties, I was asked to produce and direct two, one-hour films for a major-network series. For the first film, along with all the other directors in the series, I was put on staff and paid well for twenty weeks of acting as director and producer. All the general organizing and the postproduction work were done within the station building. When it came time to do the second film, the station was undergoing various problems and asked me to take on the film as an independent production. This meant a total budget was fixed, and the onus was on me to bring the film in on that budget. At the end of the day, I came out with maybe a third more money having independently produced, rather than having worked as gun for hire. OK, maybe there was a greater responsibility and a higher price to pay for failure, but the risk was worth it.

However, once more, there is the knowledge that when you're paid off, that's it. You've been paid well, but that's the end of the story. Then you sit down over your coffee and strudel and start thinking, what if I had part of the equity in the film? What if I actually owned the film rights? Which brings us to the major part of the chapter, how to maximize your returns when you own the film.

Making Money from Your Own Films

The theory of maximizing profits from your own films is very simple. All you have to do is bring them before the largest audience who is willing to pay you good money for the privilege of seeing your latest film. You can do this in two ways. By using a professional distributor or by self-distribution. There are pros and cons to both, and only you can judge which will be the best course to follow.

The Professional Distributor

When does the question of employing a distributor come up? Either when you totally own the film or when you have distribution rights for major territories. This latter situation usually happens when you've been involved in a coproduction, and your partners have taken the distribution rights to territories A, B, and C and left you the rest of the world.

By and large, professional distributors don't have a very good press. They are customarily scorned, badmouthed, and looked upon with deep distrust. Together with lawyers, they are often seen as carnivorous sharks, or lying con men and women. As my friend Robert Stone put it, "No matter what your film makes, you'll never see a dime. Well, maybe a dime but little else." My own partner, David, is very much of this opinion, having had a very bad experience with a distributor who made a lot of money on David's films but never paid him a penny.

But maybe it depends on whom you ask. My friend Monique swears by her distributor, and tears of gratitude come to her eyes when she thinks what her distributor has done for her. And in my own case, I've been very lucky in having a distributor whom I trust, who has become a friend, and who now and then actually makes me some money.

How do you find a distributor? Mostly, you ask professional friends, and if that doesn't help, you begin making inquiries at film festivals and film markets, where they are to be found in their dozens. And if you are involved in pitching a project or have a film actually in a film festival, don't worry. The distributor will find you. This happened to me after I pitched in Barcelona. A very pleasant man came up and introduced himself, and we chatted for half an hour about how he worked with clients and what he had to offer them. The only thing that worried me was that he was too nice and had no horns. I was at the stage where I was looking for a distributor, and he had approached me at the right time. However, after that, I did what we might call due diligence. I asked him for the names of five or six people who'd worked with him. I also asked around friends. On all sides, he came out tops. People told me he was honest and trustworthy and got their films widely circulated. That was fine for me, so I joined up and never looked back.

After your film has been shown at a few film festivals, you'll probably also find that distributors will be contacting you out of the blue. They will praise your film to the skies and promise you the moon if you sign up with them. That's a legitimate approach, and you never know, they may be for real. However, before signing any contract with them, you must do a thorough check as to who they are, who's worked with them, and whether they're satisfied.

In trying to decide whether to employ a professional distributor or self-distribute, you have to weigh the pros and cons very carefully. The main advantages of a professional distribution company is that distribution is its *main job*, and it may have the sweep, range, and ability to reach many worldwide and diverse markets that are usually beyond your own abilities. To enable you to understand the picture more precisely, I asked the Canadian distributor J. Gary Gladman of Octapixx to outline for me how his company works and what it offers the filmmaker.

We focus on broadcast and home video markets across the globe. We have sales representatives and subdistributors in most territories, particularly throughout Europe, the Near East, Middle East, and Far East. Also Japan, Australia, New Zealand, and Africa.

While we have been attending the major markets throughout the years (MIPTV, MIPDOC, NATPE, Sportel Monaco, and others), we also attend many film festivals (Hot Docs, History Makers, Wildscreen, Medimed, Factual Producers, and so forth) not only to buy titles but also particularly to meet with broadcasters who are in a "buying mood."

As much as we attend and exhibit at these markets and festivals, our ongoing marketing is on a daily basis to over three thousand broadcasters with whom we stay in regular contact and communication. The trade shows are important for us to meet and greet our customers, but the real deals are negotiated in everyday life, between shows, on a regular basis. At markets, our best sales tools are our sales sheets (also referred to as *one-sheets*). We often make a poster when we launch a new series, but the buyers are given one-sheets, which they use for reference when they get back to their home office. We also send marketing e-mails on a consistent basis.

Gary then outlined to me how he chose which broadcaster to approach first with a new show. The answer had to do with what kind of material the broadcaster had been airing in the past.

We start with the national free-to-air broadcasters or terrestrial channels, as they tend to pay to highest license fees. Of course, we simultaneously present our new titles to our stable of home video (DVD) publisher/distributors in each market. Only when we feel we have exhausted all of our free-TV sources do we move to the cable and satellite networks. . . . When we think there are opportunities for a title to win an award, we will enter it into film festivals.

Of course, what interests you as a filmmaker is how much money the distributor thinks he or she can make for you. You want to know what performance targets the distributor has in mind and sales figures for similar shows the company has handled in the past.

This is a question we are asked all the time by producers. While we would very much like to give them some figures, we feel it would be dishonest to guess at the sales we may do for a particular series . . . though we can conjure them up as well as anybody else. Most distributors know that every documentary film, drama series, movie-of-the-week, et cetera, has a life of its own. How will the viewing public respond? What will the acquisition people think of the subject matter? Is there an appropriate time slot available? Will the film be licensed to a major channel or a small digital channel? All those questions, and many more, have to be answered country-by-country, to end up with a somewhat accurate forecast—a monstrous task.

If you go ahead and link up with a professional distributor, make sure, as I have already mentioned, that you do *due diligence.* That means you contact other people who've worked with the distributor and get their opinions of the company's honesty, reliability, and ability to bring in results. You also try to put a cap on what the company wants to take for direct distribution costs, as this is a slippery item that can cost you a lot of money. Finally, I suggest you limit your contract to a year or two years to see how things turn out. If results appear fine, you renew. If results or relations are problematic, or you think another distributor could have done a better job, your hands are free to try elsewhere.

Sometimes, you may make a film that you know from the start will appeal to special interest groups, such as gay-rights communities, African Americans, Jews, or Christians. It might be worthwhile to seek out specialist distributors who have a wide experience of targeting specific audiences. If your film is mainly of interest to women, you might ask Women Make Movies to act as a distributor. If you are targeting minorities and discussing questions of race, California Newsreel might be for you. Again, if your film concerns Israel or deals with Jewish topics, you might turn to the National Archives for Jewish Film at Brandeis University to help you get the film out.

Self-distribution

Only a few years ago, the key method of getting your film seen was to use the professional distributor. Then came the revolution or, rather, a series of multirevolutions and explosions. Since the 1980s, we have joyfully entered the blazing new era of the VHS, DVD, Internet, Facebook, Twitter, the growth of film markets, and film festivals, home rental, VOD, and more. Suddenly, a mass of new options has opened up for us independent filmmakers. Like the pillar of fire before the Children of Israel in the wilderness, self-distribution, despised for so many years, has now become the guiding light for us, showing us finally how to make a buck or two from our years of filmic labor and nights of editing endeavor.

The searchlights of old Hollywood used to light up the skies. If they were now to project a guiding mantra onto the clouds, what would it be? Probably "Publicity! Publicity! Reach your widest audience, and sell your film to the widest audience possible." What does that mean when we come down to earth? It means you have to get the film out there by all means available. Let people know it exists. Let them know why they must see it. Give them that message, and they'll come running. How do you do that? By utilizing and combining any and all of the following:

- Film markets
- Film festivals
- The Internet, appearances, and circulars
- Theatrical screenings
- Amazon and video on demand

However, before getting involved in any of the above, you should prepare a publicity, information, and marketing package. This should include a DVD copy of the film, your résumé, a one-page description of the film, a color flier, photos from the film, postcards descriptions of the film, a poster, and reviews. You can then draw on and distribute these items as and when it seems appropriate. Both the one-pager and the flier are extremely important, particularly for distribution at film markets and film festivals, and you should make them as hard hitting and as attractive as you can. I've set out an example for you at the end of this chapter.

Film Markets

The expansion and growth of documentary film markets are recent trends that can be really helpful to you in selling your completed program. I've already mentioned the markets in terms of seeking finance, but they can also be useful in making sales. The most important of them are

- Hot Docs, Toronto
- IDFA, Amsterdam
- Leipzig, Germany
- MIPDOC, Cannes
- European Film Market, Berlin
- IFP, New York

- Medimed, Spain
- Sunny Side of the Doc, France
- Thessaloniki Doc Market, Greece
- East Silver Doc Market, Europe

The point of the market is to meet someone who will license your film for a TV or theatrical showing or take it up for DVD distribution. The markets used to be fun. You could schmooze, drink, and occasionally interest someone in your films. That has all changed. Many of them are now wild, free-for-all occasions where it is difficult to get any work done. Also, since the recent economic turndown, fewer buyers and network executives attend, and even then, they are reluctant to open their purses, seeing the occasion merely as a boozing junket.

All the markets work under different rules, but all require a fairly substantial enrollment fee. While some markets are just an open fairground, others, like Medimed and Leipzig, have made it easier for the seller. You submit your film to a panel. If it is accepted, then your film goes into the market video library and gets a write-up and description in the market catalogue. Buyers and distributors can read about your film and then view it in the library. You yourself can also urge the buyers to go see your work of art.

What is very important is to obtain a list of the market participants long before the due date. You then try to contact potential buyers in order to set up a meeting at the market. Without this preliminary work and investment, your time at the market can well be wasted.

Film Festivals

Having a film accepted for a festival is always a pleasure. With luck, you also get an expenses-paid invitation to come. There are parties. You meet other filmmakers. There is often good food and wine, and the ego gets positively caressed. All this is to the good. Yet, how much success at festivals really helps your sales and career as a filmmaker is another question.

On the positive side, having your film shown at a festival can create a buzz. People talk about it. It may get some good reviews that you can use in publicity. Success in a large festival like Sundance or Berlin may arouse interest from a television station or a theatrical distributor. Again, someone may be struck by your style and ingenuity and decide you are just the director they've been looking for. Festival certificates look good on your wall, and golden-prize statues in your office impress potential sponsors. To this day, I still have a bronze traffic light on my desk that was awarded to me at a film festival on road safety. And being able to say your film was shown at Hot Docs certainly does no harm to your résumé.

These days, festivals are sprouting up in every city, town, and hamlet. In the past, having a cathedral in your vicinity was the necessary qualification for allowing you to call yourself a city. In the future, the criterion may be proof of hosting a film festival. Not only large cities get in the act. Look around, and you can see that scarcely a day goes by without villages like Little Wadlington in the Marsh or Westcliff-by-the-Water announcing they are having a film festival. And why not! One has to live and let live. But on a serious level, this means you have to distinguish between the important festivals that help you to advance sales or rentals of your film and those that are just for fun. Off the cuff, I would say the seven or eight most serious documentary festivals for English-language films are Sundance, Toronto, Berlin, Sheffield, Margaret Mead, Hot Springs, Doclands (Ireland), Docfest (New York), Full Frame, and SilverDocs.

These festivals are, however, very competitive, and acceptance is not easy. Often, quite-high fees are also demanded for mere submission, and on top of that, you have to budget in travel, hotel, and food. This means you have to be very self-critical in analyzing what benefits the festival can really bring you if you are accepted.

Sometimes, it may make more sense businesswise to apply to a small specialty festival rather than one of the more well-known and grandiose ones. By specialty festivals, I mean those that emphasize a particular theme or are interested in a particular genre. If I had a film dealing with human rights, I might apply to Amnesty International Film Festival. If my film dealt with jazz, I might apply to the Denver Jazz Film Festival. Again, your film on the gay experience might be just the right film for Queerdoc or the London Lesbian and Gay Film Festival, while your film on Jewish humorists from New York could well fit in to the Boston Jewish Film Festival or Washington Jewish Film Festival.

There are two other advantages to screening in one of the specialty festivals. First, they occasionally pay for the screening or for your personal appearance as a speaker. This could earn you $300 to $400 per festival. If you appear at four of five similar festivals, that could mean $2,000 in your pocket. Possibly even more important, if you appear as a speaker, the audience may often want to buy DVDs of the film from you on the spot.

So if you've made a film on say folk music in Ireland and manage to sell twelve DVDs, at say $30 each (a not unreasonable sum), you are $360 up.

These days, finding the right festival is extremely easy. To start with, you might want to note that the Association of Independent Video and Filmmakers (AIVF) puts out a very useful guide to international film-and-video festivals. Check the organization's Web site. You can also get a long list of festivals and their specialties by simply searching "documentary film festivals" on Google. For festival updates, withoutabox. com is also a useful address for telling you what's happening on the festival circuit.

The Internet, the Web, Appearances, and Circulars

Again, I emphasize, your goal is to seek maximum publicity for your film and let people know why they should buy, rent, or screen it publicly. The Internet, personal appearances, and circulars all help towards that end. But you must keep your eye on the ball. Publicity is fine, but it doesn't exist in a vacuum. Its aim is to produce sales. Web sites don't always do that, at least not always directly. Their real importance maybe in announcing your work and acting as general PR. With the spread of the Internet, Facebook, and Twitter, we are all into self-publicity, and if we can harness the opportunities offered by these trends, they may be able to help our films. I say maybe because I am not totally convinced.

A lot has been written about film streaming and putting parts of your film on YouTube. However, I know no one who has made much money this way. First, in reality the viewing of net streaming is really quite low. In a recent survey, investigators found that whereas the people watched fifty hours standard television per month, they only watched four hours on the net. This may be skewed as more people tend to turn to the Internet, but it does make you face facts. Secondly, after making an extensive viewing of the literature and talking to many filmmakers, I've found little evidence that producers have made over $4,000 from the Internet. Nevertheless, you might note that many projects end up as QuickTime files for circulation during the postproduction process and for help with film-festival entries.

While researching this chapter, I noticed that a company called Snag-Films had started an online service allowing documentaries to be shown free. Well, that's fine if your main purpose is to get your political or propaganda message out. Or you just want to build up your reputation. Not so great if you want to make money. So, publicity yes, major sales no. Yet, technology and ideas change so fast, that in a year or so, I may well be proved wrong on this point.

Contrary to Internet streaming, setting up a personal Web site can be extremely beneficial for particular films and for your company as a whole. I am totally for the idea. Your Web site can provide wide publicity for you personally and for your organization and can also help you sell your films.

Sometimes, people construct their own Web sites to save money. In this case, I would advise you to get it done professionally, because it's going to be your calling card to the world and will often represent people's first view of who you are. So here, money well spent is money well saved.

The contents of people's Web sites vary enormously, but the following seem to me basic content suggestions for most filmmakers' Web sites.

- Broadcast and location dates of your latest film
- Story, reviews, and other information about particular films
- Stills from the film
- Possibly short extracts from the film
- Information on how to purchase the film from you. This is vital.
- Notes for particular interest groups
- General information on your company and its history
- Information on other films you have made and their availability
- Notes on future films you are contemplating

According to your particular situation, you may want to add other areas. That's up to you. The basic thing is to make your Web site punchy, attractive, and easily accessible.

Of all the information you provide, the note about how to buy the film may be the most important. If you can sell the film (and your other films) from your Web site, you cut out all the middlemen, and your profit ration is much higher.

But making your Web site is only the beginning. You have to publicize it by all means possible, via film markets, film festivals, notes to TV stations, individual circulars, and others. It's a mine of information, but you have to work hard to get people to look at it. One trick is to see if there is any special-interest group that would be interested in your films. You make films about environmental problems? If so, find out the group interested in the subject, and let them know of your Web site. You make films about human rights? Ditto. You make films about health problems and alternative medicine? Fine. Get on immediately to all those multiple health organizations that exist everywhere. Let them know you exist, and your films may help them and be of interest to them.

Dennis Smith, an Australian, made a controversial political film about the local building industry. He writes:

> The national broadcasters backed away from it, and we in turn asked the relevant union to back the film. They did, and we used their money to construct a Web site from which you can view parts of the film, download the whole film, buy a DVD, book a public screening, or become a part of the debate. We used a viral marketing campaign using the young filmmaker on radio, in meetings, presentations, and so forth, as well as employing someone to link our site to other union sites, green sites, social action groups, and the like.
>
> The campaign was successful in that it got the word out there, and we sold via downloads and DVDs, which returned monies to us in addition to our fees . . .
>
> Currently, we are sitting on our hands. We have other films that are broadly saleable to special-interest and niche groups. We need to build a site to conjure interest in these and to link our sites to those of special-interest and niche groups.

Dennis added, in his letter to me, that there was no pot of gold at the end of the rainbow, but the returns weren't bad. Other filmmakers with whom I've corresponded have told me they've made between $10,000 to $15,000 on direct sales through their Web sites. The potential is there.

Dennis mentions how he used the young filmmaker on radio, in meetings, and presentations. These are all words to bear in mind. Radio and TV will give you exposure. Exposure will give you more screenings and sales. Contact your local radio and TV stations, and tell them what you are up to and what you've been doing, and you provide them with DVD copies of your film. You appear and plug your film for all you're worth. The same applies to the local newspapers. You contact their appropriate critic, who may be in news, current affairs, or the arts, tell him or her about your film, and supply him or her with your press kit.

Finally, we come to schools, universities, and special-interest groups. Contact them, send them your circulars and DVD, and let them know you have a film that might interest them, that you are available to accompany screenings, and that the film is also available for purchase for their libraries.

Again, the bottom line is you don't need a middleman to sell your film. Do some thinking, identify your market, and then get to it. A friend of mine made a film about the Sydney Opera House. Since then, the film has been screened on TV, but, more important, thousands of DVD copies of the film have been sold through the Opera House shop and many more to worldwide museums and universities.

Theatrical Screenings

Every so often, the newspapers proclaim the box-office triumphs of documentary films. So we hear that *Super Size Me*, the attack on Big Macs, made $11 million at the box office, as did *Winged Migration*. We are in awe when we note that *Fahrenheit 9/11* pulled in $119 million and give a nod of congratulations when we note that *Capturing the Friedmans* brought in over three million and *Trembling Before G-d* collected a very sweet $600,000 from theatrical viewers. And then we usually react in two ways. We are overcome by admiration for the filmmakers but are also quite envious. Why, we ask ourselves, couldn't that be us pulling in the dollars or, as Damon Runyon put it, the glistening semollions?

My answer is that a unique combination of circumstances accounts for the success of most of these films and that I suspect the boom is over. If you reckon that probably over ten thousand documentaries are made a year in the United States, and maybe only three or four of them get decent returns from a theatrical release, you see how high are the odds stacked against success. The situation seems even bleaker when you take in to account the disappointments surrounding some of the most-hyped documentaries of the last few years. *Taxi to the Dark Side* won a documentary Oscar but failed to draw in audiences, while Errol Morris's film on Abu Ghraib, *Standard Operating Procedure*, only brought in a paltry $210,000. It seems as if in this day and age, audiences are mostly content to stay home and watch their documentaries on television.

For a number of years, I took notes about theatrical documentary releases in the States. What emerged is that though many of them, such as *Wasn't That a Time*, received great reviews, very few did more than just cover the expenses of the showing. When a film does have a major success, such as Werner Herzog's Antarctica film *Encounters at the End of the World* or *Touching the Void*, it's usually because of special reasons such as being made by a well-known director or providing a fascinating unknown story shot in a unique location or being totally the first of its kind.

Does that mean there is no money to be had from a theatrical release and that pushing your film in that direction is not worth the effort? Well, not necessarily. The showing itself may not bring in much cash, but there maybe ancillary benefits. For one thing, your film becomes eligible for an Oscar nomination. Secondly, the publicity obtained may help you in your wider sales pitches and film operations. You may be able to sell a considerable number of DVDs at the showings. Universities and schools may hear of you and ask you to speak and screen. And finally, local individuals or business corporations seeking to make a film may decide you are just the director and producer they need.

So a case can be made for a theatrical showing, but if you are heading in that direction, examine the finances very carefully. What are the costs of renting the theater? How much will advertising on radio, TV, and newspapers put you out of pocket? What are the realistic expected returns? If you crunch the numbers and are happy, then good luck to you. If not, save your money for your next film, which you know will be so incredible it will really have them circling the block for tickets and rolling in the aisles.

Amazon and Video on Demand (VOD)

The underlying message running through all of the above paragraphs is that there is money to be made by direct selling of DVDs to the public. I've outlined various ways to do this, but three other main ways are selling via Amazon, video on demand (VOD), and licensing the film to a DVD distributor.

All work in basically the same way. They take your film, put it on their sites, or give it to their sales agents and wait for results. The two problems are publicity and minimal returns. No one will turn to Amazon or ask for your film on VOD unless they've heard of it. The publicity operation is left to you. The second problem is you may only receive a half or a third, or less, of the retail sale price of your film. Still, as the old saw has it, twenty per cent of something is better than sixty per cent of nothing.

The Flier

I mentioned the importance of the flier in drawing attention to your film once it has been completed. Below is an extract from the flier of a recent film of mine that may help you to see how these things are designed and written.

Flier: *Stalin's Last Purge*

In discussing the flier with the designer, I opted for very bold red lettering with the film's name superimposed over a black-and-white photograph of Stalin. Underneath the photo, we see the following:

> He saw enemies everywhere and decided to destroy them all in one great last purge. First the Jews, then his secret service, then his political rivals.
>
> But would he succeed?

The flier itself contained quite a lot of information. I gave a lot of thought to the opening paragraphs, which had to arouse the interest of the reader, and to the last paragraph that had to ram the story home.

> Shot in Russia, Israel, and the United States, this one-hour documentary special takes us back to the USSR in the late forties. It is a USSR where Stalin reigns supreme. After the devastating war against the Nazis in which over twenty million citizens have died, Stalin is seen as King, God, and Messiah rolled into one.
>
> But the cold war is unfolding, and Stalin's paranoia is increasing. He sees real and imaginary enemies everywhere but plans a final campaign to destroy them all. Once more he will let loose the terror. Once more there will be the cry in the night, the knock on the door, and the bullet in the neck. . . .
>
> [Final paragraph] Much of the material used in *Stalin's Last Purge* has only recently become available. The opening of the Soviet archives in the 1990s uncovered a treasure trove of secret information about the USSR. These revelations, together with the new interviews and rarely seen archive materials, present the viewer with an unforgettable and riveting story about Stalin and about life and terror in the former Soviet police state.

It's useful to remember one key thing about fliers, that *look* may be more important than *language*. So make it stand out. Make it bold. Make it fly!

13. Notes from the Front

WHILE I WAS PREPARING THIS book, many friends and acquaintances took time off to either write to me or sit down and discuss with me many of the issues we've been talking about. Their thoughts and advice were invaluable as they updated me as to what was going on in the field and why they had made their documentary choices and informed me about their struggles to make a living. Here and there, I've managed to introduce a few of their comments, but mostly I had to leave them out due to the pressures of space. However, I told my editor, I really did want to include some of their voices and feelings, so with boundless generosity, he's allowed me to finish off the book with what I call "Notes from the Front."

Film School

The two years I spent at the Stanford Documentary Film Program opened up the world to me. The small class size (eleven students) encouraged strong friendships and professional relationships that have lasted over a decade since. I felt privileged to be taught by Jan Krawitz and Kris Samuelson, two talented professors and inspiring people. I saw a bunch of great work in documentary history and various colloquiums and learned a ton about production through the project-based hands-on curriculum (all the students churn out short film after short film and play various production roles on other students' films). In short, my experience at Stanford changed my life.

Mark Becker, United States

The New York University film school was rather small when I came in 1969 . . . maybe three hundred students. The teachers were good, and George Stoney was a treasure and particularly inspiring. What worked for me was the whole package. Access to equipment, classes on how to put film together and operate the equipment at a time when I was really motivated to learn. . . . I don't remember anything outstanding from a single lecture, but having access to teachers after class is where I learned a lot, where I got advice for projects. They were more like coaches than professors.

Jim Brown, United States

What did they fail to teach me in film school? That the most often occurring job title is "son-in-law." Two: never make enemies. The *putz* you scream at today maybe listening to your pitch tomorrow. Three: all other things being equal, ambition and drive tend to trump talent.

I also believe that filmmakers, whether students or professionals, are afflicted by irrational optimism about finances and the belief that "since we're all friends," a letter of agreement is not necessary.

Last words of wisdom? For young people, get a mentor with whom you can discuss your work with candor and honesty, someone you know and trust so well that neither you nor he or she will be overly concerned with hurt feelings. If your mentor can introduce you to other people working in the field, so much the better.

Henry Breitrose, United States

You should major in English, or art, or history. You can learn this technical stuff in your spare time. Study film on your own. You just want to know something when you get here. Having some perspective in your head helps, and most of all, find a good partner.

Mark Benjamin, United States

Starting Out

After finishing film school, I teamed up with two other students from my class and decided to develop some projects. We won a few awards at film festivals and started developing a project called *Fahimeh's Story.*

In order to sell this film to a broadcaster, I decided to make a promo video. I borrowed a camera from a friend and started shooting some of the events in Fahimeh's life. I wanted to see how the film would work and what potential it would have. After a few weeks of research and shooting, I asked my friend Axel to help me cut a promo for the project. After getting the promo ready, I approached a few producers in Brisbane, including my old professor, Ian Lang. . . . Ian was very interested and had a lot of qualities that were unique and outstanding. After teaming up with Ian, we pitched the idea to SBS. They loved the idea almost immediately. The problem was access to budget. From the time I pitched the idea to SBS to the time that I could get my hands on the budget took about fourteen months.

Faramarz K-Rahber, Australia

Like many film students, I wanted to work in the film industry as an editor. However, my interviews with the film-production companies shattered my dream. I remember when the head of the editing department told me, "Forget that! We would not employ a woman to work in postproduction. Women are only good at doing the job of a production assistant." Another executive told me, "I'll only employ you to be my personal assistant." I finished up working as a freelance editor on small-budget documentaries and instructional videos.

Gipsy Chang, editor, Hong Kong

I was living in England, working as a lawyer, but wanted to take time off to go to Jerusalem to do a film about children on kibbutzim, the Israeli communal farms. So I was in the mood for action but with no idea how to bring something off. I then got a phone call from a friend who worked as an editor at the BBC. He wanted to make a film about deserts and had a silent Bolex camera that took hundred-foot spools. He had also collected about five thousand feet of loose ends of film that remained over when the cameraperson had almost, but not quite, finished shooting his four-hundred-foot reels. He thought we could make a shoestring film together, with both of us directing and shooting and him editing. So we printed cards that said "Universal Documentaries" and went off to Israel to do a film about desert water problems, which we later sold to the BBC.

A few years later, I found myself teaching two courses at Haifa University, a new Israeli university that had only been in the academic business a few years but that was about to embark on a huge building program. One day I thought, "Why not," and went to see the head of public relations. "You may not know it," I said, "but I think you need a film to show to your donors." "Let me think about it," she said. Two weeks after, I had a contract for my first independent film. The budget was $10,000, and I managed to hold on to $4,000 after everything was paid for.

Alan Rosenthal, Israel

My wife, Elisabeth, and I made our first film somewhere after the Yom Kippur war in Israel. That first film was called *My Father's House*. CBS bought it, which is a kind of joke. I'm twenty-seven, and CBS buys my first film. It was not a very good film but heartfelt. The idea for the film came from my friend Larry Price. It helped that the film was about something that nobody had any sense of—mystical Judaism. Nobody could spell Kabbalah in those days. The questions brought up in the film were interesting. CBS bought it, paid us, and broadcast it. And right after the film, CBS gave us another assignment, *Twice Promised Land*, which was about the Palestinian-Israeli conflict. We interviewed Israelis and Palestinians, asked them the same questions, and intercut the material. We created a dialogue. It was lucky for us, a couple of kids in our twenties; we got a good review in the *New York Times* from John O'Connor, which was a break. That was 1974.

Mark Benjamin, United States

Taking Off

I studied at Griffith Film School and graduated with a Bachelor of Communications in television production and media and communication studies. I made some films and worked for different companies but had a very strong yearning to go out on my own. I wanted to tell my own stories . . . so I started my own production company, Fury Productions. It was a tough call. I was seen as emerging and inexperienced. It was a very hard time in such a competitive and underresourced industry. I had to earn money on the side building Web sites to get through—a second skill never goes astray. But I persisted and made sure I attended as many industry and social functions as I could and, most important, developed a broad but strong slate of projects to pitch.

Of importance, I visited other successful production companies in Australia and looked at how they operated, what were their business models, how did they operate, and how did they survive, etc. I then modeled my own business on them. I also made a lot of mistakes during that time. I optioned projects incorrectly. I handled some industry relationships badly and spent some time developing projects that were simply not going to get up. But I learned from these mistakes. Overall, I was really not prepared for these real-life industry issues through university. It was a real learn-on-the-job situation. I now have a good lawyer. I treat colleagues carefully and really study the market before developing projects to a pitching level.

After two years of what I could compare to climbing Everest, I got my first television commission on a two-hour social-history project. I had teamed up with a highly experienced and award-winning team, which was a real winner for the commissioning editors. Other commissions have followed, and today I really feel I am on my way. But I know well enough I have a long way to go. I am really still only at the foothills of Everest. Thank goodness my motto is onwards and upwards.

Veronica Fury, Australia

If development as a filmmaker's meant anything to me, it's been learning to listen instead of talk or, worse, preach. It's taken me years to listen, but it's the greatest gift you could give to someone who's never been heard.

I was terrified the subjects wouldn't talk to me. Now I'm trying to work out how to shut them up. I've had to learn to understand other people's suffering without letting it burn me up. I've had to become professionalized in some ways to convince myself I'm not a do-gooder parachuting in and bailing out as soon as I've assuaged my guilt.

Don't be a doco maker if you're not the witness type. Don't do it if all you really want is to show people The Deep and Complex Mystery That Is Me. And definitely don't shoot a thing if all your right reasons are about making people feel guilty about something, rather than helping people understand things they never did before. Preaching to the converted is just cheap propaganda to make yourself feel better, and we can do better than that.

Lots of jobs need you to be a team player, and that's sort of true for documentary. But, personally, I've always liked individual sports. It's satisfying for me to go into a brand-new situation, with nothing but my wits, and the least kit I can get away with. But I really need separate eyes to tease out the best story for the edit—and I couldn't do that without my partner, Judith. My closest friends and family have mostly come from documentary.

Ian Lang, Australia

I thought I would be able to work in the industry, but I was kind of naïve. Cal Arts is not a business school, and there were no classes that offered me skills in how to market my work, how to write a grant proposal, how to distribute a film, etc. I found that students who did extremely well after Cal Arts already had those skills from previous jobs or had been born into a family that was wealthy. They were savvy at marketing and distributing their work and had been born into a network of people in the industry.

I was passionate about wanting to represent what mainstream media didn't offer, which is the story of failed American dreams. I have never screened anything on POV. *AKA Kathe* was considered but didn't make the final cut. I'd put about $15,000 of my own money into *AKA Kathe*. I got about half of that back in paid screenings and educational video sales. But the real cash came in getting university jobs and residencies. The film gave me some teaching gigs, but I didn't do as well in marketing the film as I should have.

Minda Martin, United States

Pitching, Funding, Contracts, and Marketing

Pitching in many cases is a junket for the commissioning editor, who simply wants to escape the cold English winter for some warm weather in Australia. When we pitched *The Diplomat* (about the exiled East Timorese leader Jose Ramos Horta) back in 1998 at a pitching forum in Brisbane, a well-known BBC commissioning editor said to us, "Where is East Timor, and what would our audience [in England] care about a liberation struggle on the other side of the world?"

Things have improved in ten years but only a little. This year, I pitched a project on the Western Sahara and the world's longest-running refugee camp. Interest was shown by U.S. networks and European broadcasters, but the BBC was only mildly interested.

Pitching is useful because you instantly see what interest exists out there, and then you capitalize on that information. This leads to further meetings, which open up a dialogue with broadcasters that eventually (hopefully) results in a presale.

I've had a mixed experience with distributors, some good, some bad. With some, you have to read the riot act to them so that they produce figures and balance sheets, etc. Others dutifully give you half-yearly reports. Some of them go broke and owe you thousands of dollars that you never see. But occasionally you meet an angel. Boutique distributors who have a limited catalogue and rally hard at pushing and promoting your film. For example, Films Transit, which organized an international premiere for *Molly and Mobarak* so that it opened at the Margaret Mead Film Festival.

Tom Zubrycki, Australia

My experience with distributors has been mixed. With one distributor, I have had to constantly fight for contractually mandated quarterly statements and payment. The others have paid promptly with a full account of who bought or rented the film. My biggest complaint with nontheatrical distributors is that they typically don't advocate for specific films in their catalogue. It is more of a passive distribution whereby they put the film in a catalogue and hope it sells. A perspicacious producer will typically do a lot of legwork of identifying potential users and pass that on to the distributor. But that can become a full-time job, and it is, unfortunately, time that I don't have.

I have twice terminated contracts with distributors who failed to live up to their end of the bargain.

Jan Krawitz, United States

The most common problem I see in negotiating copyright or contracts is that people tend to believe that they cannot understand the contracts and that because someone is a lawyer, he must know what he is talking about. In quite a few cases I've worked on here in Singapore, the in-house counsel is skilled in a different area of law from contract law or copyright law as it pertains to media use.

In those situations, mine and the students' general knowledge were often equal to the lawyer's, in some cases better.

In those cases, we've had repeatedly to explain our legal needs and why the contract doesn't meet it. Maybe American contracts are different, but in all the contracts given to me by legal departments here in Singapore and Hong Kong, I have not seen one yet that states what rights the filmmaker does have, only the limitations and obligations to the company.

Nicole Lorraine Draper, Singapore

My biggest problem is funding. Broadcasters, especially the BBC, will commission my ideas but only fund around 40 percent of the budget. So I have to go shopping for the rest in America and Europe, often a grueling job and not what I'm good at. Coproducers have usually behaved well, but putting in different languages can be a trial. To save money, I also find myself shooting a lot of stuff myself, which is fun but risky.

My only pitching experience was at Amsterdam. Lots of good feedback but zero money. I know others have had more profitable experiences.

My main beef with broadcasters is to do with sluggish decision making. Americans can be especially frustrating due to towering hierarchies as they wait for superiors to give them a go-ahead.

Leslie Woodhead, England

I have very little experience in getting projects off the ground. People have always come to me with proposals to collaborate, rather than vice versa. My only advice, for what it's worth, is that turnover, not only in commissioning editors but also heads of department, is so rapid in our industry that no one should ever discard a project. Whenever someone in a position to make decisions resigns or is sacked, simply represent it (after a decent interval) to his or her successor. Also remember that commissioning editors have a very short attention span. Three paragraphs is about all they can absorb. A good way of practicing is to (literally) write a press release. It tells everyone what the point of the film is. And to do it, you will have to unclutter your mind wonderfully.

Jerry Kuehl, England

I think that every successful documentary filmmaker, driven by passion or not, realizes that the film has no impact if no one sees it, and [the film] loses passion and relevance if it is aimed at the least-common denominator to achieve the maximum audience.

Henry Breitrose, United States

All of my films have been funded by multiple small grants from a variety of agencies and/or foundations. However, I have never received a single grant that could pay for the entire production. Like most independent documentarians, the film is funded by cobbling together many different funding sources.

The biggest "sea change" in recent years is that you have to spend money before you can raise money. It's now the case that a trailer is required in order to get funding for a project. When projects were shot on film, this was never a condition for funding the production side of a film, although a work-in-progress [report] was typically required for a postproduction grant. These days, there are very few grants for the research and development stage, and most production grants require a trailer. This means that the filmmaker is required to go out-of-pocket to undertake a preliminary shoot that will result in a competitive fund-raising trailer.

Jan Krawitz, United States

If a documentary is released properly, not only for academy consideration but also with a goal to making money, and the doc has an appeal for wide audiences, I believe you can make a profit. Not *Pirates* kind of money but rather the *Penguins* kind. The distributor has to be willing to spend some dollars, to have a solid PR and marketing campaign in place, and to have patience, since it's mostly word of mouth that will make it happen. If you leave the film in the theater for one week only, it won't happen.

In the case of *Cowboy Del Amor*, we had a limited run for Academy purposes, and people who came loved the film and told their friends. Word of mouth started to spread, but the film was already out of the theaters by the time the word was out, and people didn't have a chance to see the movie. It was very frustrating because we knew how much audiences enjoyed the film at festivals and at other screenings and how we could fill the theaters if the distributors and theater owners were not willing to give us a chance or have financial patience.

Showtime Inc. bought the film, and it had an extremely successful run, also on Netflix. So you always make up for it on the small
screen if the film is appealing.

Michèle Ohayon, United States

Regarding theatrical documentaries: yes, I've done this, and my new
film is about to be released theatrically, as is the one I'm beginning
production on. Outside Michael Moore, who is in a class by himself,
theatrical docs are not money-making propositions. They enhance
your status as a director, thus enabling you to get money for your
next film more easily. They raise the profile of your film, which increases TV ratings when it's broadcast and DVD sales. But virtually
nobody I know has ever made money on it. Whatever a film makes
at the box office is just about what it costs to release it and then
some. Beyond your advance, you're not likely to see any money,
even with a hit film. That's the sad truth as I've seen it. Regardless,
we'd all kill to get a theatrical release because of the prestige. In our
celebrity culture, fame (even minor documentary-world fame) is the
most valuable currency of all.

Robert Stone, United States

Documentaries can make money theatrically at the box office, but it
usually takes a special set of circumstances to build a national and
international awareness of the film and just the right approach and
subject matter. I would say it's more the exception than the rule.

Jim Brown, United States

I can't make the same thing twice. I could never do formula, which
is what investors like. They want you to make the same thing again
and again, and I can't do that. I continue to make films that revisit
my past, to understand what I couldn't while growing up, such
as living in poverty, living with an alcoholic parent, living with
displacement and shame. . . . I seem to be drawn to people who have
lost hope so much that they don't even remember their dreams. So
often we see in the mainstream media only stories of the successful.
But what about the millions of stories that have failed? Do they not
count? Can't we learn something from failure?

Minda Martin, United States

The Commissioning Editor and Lawyers

At the core of a successful pitch lies the ability to let a vision come to life with just a few words. Christian Bauer was a master of pitches. He told his stories in a sentence or two, sometimes in English, sometimes in German, but always with a soft voice. These two well-thought-out sentences were usually enough to kick off yet another successful production with ARTE:

1. Jewish guys have to emigrate from Germany to the United States. In Camp Ritchie, they are trained by the U.S. secret service only to return to Europe to eavesdrop on Nazis and war criminals. (*The Ritchie Boys*, 1990, Oscar shortlisted. Christian Bauer)
2. Kaefer is a high-profile event caterer in Munich covering the entire event range in Germany's prime party location. Their crew swears, sweats, loves, and cries and even marries each other. (*The True Kir Royal*, first doco-soap in French and German television)
3. Birgit is a Bavarian-born truck driver in the United States. When she falls ill with cancer, she takes an eighteen-foot truck with eighteen wheels right across the United States and Canada. (*A Female Truck Driver in the USA*)
4. A few "charming" boys enter the boarding school of the famous dome choire in the city of Regensburg and learn how to sing like angels. (*Domspatzen*, Bavarian Film Price, 2009)

ARTE is a German-French TV channel renowned for its first-time screenings and documentary productions. Hundreds of scripts and projects from hopeful filmmakers pass through the hands of commissioning editors and program directors every month. ARTE also develops and produces its own formats and new concepts. The channel is a true melting pot of cultures, visions, and creative ideas.

The decision if a project pitch is successful and the project is accepted and financed by ARTE is a somewhat more democratic process than at other networks. Generally, pitching is a hierarchical procedure. The commissioning editor needs to approve and sign on a project before another program director above him will review the project and sign on it as well. Once the signatures are in place, money becomes available for the producer, given that his or her suggested financial budget was realistic.

At ARTE, however, this decision-making process takes place on a monthly basis with not less than eight people involved: commissioning editors, program directors, and heads of departments from the French side and the German side. Together, they discuss and review all pitches before democratically deciding on a "yes" or "no" or possibly a "pending approval." The president of this conference, Christoph Hauser, must read several hundred projects every month; over the course of his career, this amounts to not less than twenty thousand projects.

So, what are the criteria for a successful pitch? For us, the commissioning editors, the three main questions are

- Why do *we* need this film? Why should ARTE finance this particular project?
- Why should we produce this film at this particular time?
- Why should it be realized in this particular format?

Pitching is a skill that can be learned. Some may find pleasure in the " elevator pitching" workshops at the annual Realscreen Summit in Washington, D.C. A hopeful producer steps into a hotel elevator where he meets his potential "decision maker with a budget." He then has five to ten floors, or de facto thirty to fifty-five seconds, to pitch his project to the decision maker and get an equally quick yes-or-no answer.

An example for a very successful pitch is Gunnar Dedio's film about executioners in western and Central Europe. His pitch perfectly followed the three golden rules:

- The title should say immediately what the film is about. "Executioners. Death has a face."
  His pitch went like this: "Executioners are the only people who have the right to kill in a civil society. So they know death. Each of them kills in a different way. Mostly at day break. The executioners now show their faces, explain their trade, and tell their life stories."
- State in the logline of your project pitch which story you want to tell—simply, directly, and short.
  "Executioners are the only people in civil society that have the license to kill. They know death. Each and every one of them kills in his own way. Mostly at sunrise. Executioners. Now they are showing their faces. Tell their stories. Explain their craft."
- Tell your story in an engaging way. Do not bore your audience to tears.

Gunnar's pitch immediately got everyone's attention. In light of such a story, it was impossible to remain indifferent.

A good pitching paper must answer the following three essential questions:

- What do you want to produce? What is the film about?
- How do you want to realize it? The visual concept is of utmost importance: have you found extraordinary archive footage? Will you make use of CGI or reenactments?
- Who are you? What have you produced in the past—what is your filmography? What references do you have? Give names and phone numbers.

Further material is highly recommended:

- You have to know the channel for which you produce. The slots, the program scheme, target groups, the ratings. Think about which value you bring to the channel, which relevance your project has for culture, for Europe, for Israel, for Brazil, or for the world. It is invaluable to be clear about the core message of the film.
- Again, what is the value of your film for the network?
- Has the story been told before? Are there new scientific facts? Has everything been told, but now *you* have found a totally new format to tell it once more?
- If you send the commissioning editors a hard copy, always remember to send it by e-mail as well and bring along a flash drive on which you can even add the teaser. Never send more than 2 MB.

A final word: take your time for good projects and for beautiful films. The great Charlie Chaplin once said, "Filmmakers should consider that on judgment day, all of their films will be shown to them one last time." Is he right? We will see. Insh'allah! It will most certainly apply to filmmakers as well as program directors, commissioning editors, and producers as well.

> Peter Gottschalk, commissioning editor, ARTE France

Dealing with commissioning editors is becoming trickier. When I first started out, in the early days of independent access to the BBC, ITV, and Channel 4, it was difficult to raise finance if you hadn't previously known these commissioning editors as colleagues in a British broadcaster or if you didn't drink in the fashionable wine bars of Islington. It was even more difficult if you had an Irish address on your company letterhead. At least, one thought, they might commission me to make a documentary about Irish politics, as those were the years of violent dispute, quaintly known as "the Troubles." But, of course, that was the last subject they'd trust an Irish filmmaker to do. There was an honourable exception for a few years in the 1980s when Jeremy Isaacs, the first chief executive of Channel 4, gave his commissioning editor for religion (!) the additional responsibility of financing or cofunding documentaries specifically about Ireland, and I benefited from this policy.

However, there is much more nervousness on behalf of commissioners these days. They often seem to prefer working with younger directors, ostensibly because they are of the generation that is used to the fast-paced techniques of MTV or the immediacy of the Internet. But it also might be because these newcomers are so grateful to have been given an opportunity and therefore are less likely to be "awkward" or "difficult" than more-experienced documentary makers with their own views on structure and style. This nervousness is probably because the commissioning editors themselves are under pressure from their superiors (or "line managers"), owing to the perceived precarious position of public-service broadcasting in the multichannel world of the twenty-first century.

Donald Taylor Black, Ireland

I have just returned from the Australian Film Institute Awards. At this gala event in Melbourne, awards were given out for best director, best editor, best cinematographer, best actors, and, of course, best film. Alas, there was no award for the "best lawyer." Indeed, no lawyer who worked on any of the films was even thanked in the acceptance speeches.

Does that mean that lawyers are an unimportant and peripheral "afterthought" for any films, including documentaries, that are being produced? At the risk of sounding like I am promoting my own profession, I can emphatically state that a good lawyer is an essential element to any film being made. A good lawyer will ensure that all the "drama" remains on the screen and not in a real-life courtroom drama if disputes arise.

So why is it important to have a savvy film lawyer on your side? An experienced lawyer will assist at every stage of the making of the film, from financing to production and also distribution and marketing.

When a film is made, certain contracts (i.e., binding agreements) need to be entered into between the production company and other parties. For example, there is the production investment agreement (PIA) between the investors in the film and the production company. The PIA sets out the obligation of the investors (namely, that they will invest money in the film) and the rights of the investors (such as their entitlement to copyright, recoupment, and profit, as well as their approval rights over various cuts of the film). The PIA will also set out the obligations of the production company, notably that the production company will deliver the film in accordance with the agreed treatment or script, within the agreed budget, and by the agreed delivery date.

The production company will also enter into an international sales-agency agreement for the international distribution of the film and also possibly one-on-one presales of the film with local distributors or broadcasters in certain territories.

One must also consider crew agreements and cast agreements in a docudrama. The writer's agreement will ensure that copyright in the treatment or script is assigned from the writer to the production company so that there is a clear chain of title. There are also release forms that need to be executed regarding interviewees, locations, archives, music, and sound.

In my role as a lawyer, I am always telling clients that one of my golden rules is, "If you think something is worth stealing, someone will think it's worth protecting." In other words, the filmmaker needs to get permission from the owner of copyright for the inclusion of even a short length of music or an obscure piece of archive footage. A filmmaker once said to me that she was only using ten seconds of Rolling Stones' music in her film so didn't think she needed to clear copyright with the music publisher or recording company. Alas, she thought the music was worth stealing, and no doubt had she used it without permission, the Rolling Stones would have thought it worth protecting!

The whole point of a written and signed contract is to give certainty to the contracting parties. So all of the above agreements are usually entered into before a single shot of footage has been taken for the film. That way, the production company can move forward knowing it has secured its investors, distribution strategy, and releases from the get-go. My role as lawyer is to make sure those agreements are fair and favorable to the filmmaker within the confines of (what is often) disparity of bargaining power between my client and the parties on the side.

Lawyers not only provide legal advice. An experienced lawyer will also act as a consultant or possibly even a confidant of the filmmaker—advising him or her on a range of nonlegal issues, such as, where to find potential investors, what commissioning editors are worth approaching, and what film-festival roll-out strategy would work best for the film. In that sense, the lawyer takes on the role of executive producer and friend-in-chief for the filmmaker.

So while there may never be an Oscar Award category for the "best lawyer," it's a wise idea to have a smart film lawyer advising you along your filmmaking journey. And when things *don't* go wrong with the contracts, you can thank your lawyer—but not too much because, after all, YOU were the one who made the great film!

Shaun Miller, lawyer, Melbourne, Australia

Cautionary Tales

Have I been screwed? Yes, creatively, on one recent occasion. It was on a project brought to me by a producer. I fell in love with the project but then demanded that I coproduce with her. She refused. I still went along as the director and had a bad experience making the film. The main falling out was at rough cut, when she demanded a narration. I virtually walked off the project. There were so many kind of creative compromises that I ended up hating the experience.

Tom Zubrycki, Australia

My two favorite lessons are these. If you tell someone they have to "review" material for approval, they feel obligated to make a change. My former boss used to swear that he'd put in one obviously horrible shot or bad edit and tell the client, "I just don't know about this thing. What do you think?" and when the review was over, they'd usually say, "I love it, but I think you're right. That [shot/edit/music] has to go." At which point, he'd stroke his beard and say, "Maybe this might work," and pull out the shot he'd been thinking about all along. And the other person would love it.

Secondly, if a client tells you he wants something fresh?! New! Pushing the boundaries! you should run fast and far. They don't know what they're talking about. They almost certainly mean safe, something my bosses will like. High expectations and no budget!

When I was working at a production house, the local police department wanted a training video and decided they wanted a fresh approach. They brought us their training scenario in a humorous format, somewhat similar to *Groundhog Day* . . . and we asked the administrative manager, "Is this really what you want us to do?" Every meeting we asked again and again, "Are you sure?" and every time they said yes. . . . In short, we went overboard to ensure that we had authority approval every step of the way.

Then the day arrived to review the first cut. After the viewing, there was a dead silence. Then the manager from the police department turned to the police rep and said, "Can I speak to you outside?" Later they came back in, and the manager said, "It's not serious enough. It makes the department look foolish." The manager gave a small nod to the fact that the police rep had been on site and had approved the takes, but he insisted that we do a major reshoot gratis.

Nicole Lorraine Draper, Singapore

Every day I'm discovering new traps I can fall into. . . . It is important to understand the workings of the industry when establishing a career. In particular, I fell into the trap of refusing to work on green-lighted projects because I was so in love with my own projects. My agent should have threatened to commit me to an asylum in a couple of instances, but they were far too polite . . . or stupid.

Have I been promised the earth? All the time. That is SOP. Agents do it. Producers do it to get you to work on their films. Producers do it to get you to sign with them. The problem is there are few rewards for telling the cautious truth. People always want to believe they will win the lottery. No one will sell lottery tickets if he tells his customers they don't stand chance.

John Fox, United States

My first full-length documentary *Sail Around Singapore* got excellent reviews. Then via government channels, a mandate came down to make three films about rapidly disappearing ethnic areas in Singapore. The mandate was clear: herald the colorful aspects of Singapore's three cultures, and I was chosen to produce the documentary about the last days of Chinatown. . . .

The ruling Peoples Action Party called the tune, and I knew there was no way that I could really deal with the old dialect-speaking groups as they were the PAP's staunchest opposition. But I still thought I could make an entertaining film with some integrity—at least more exciting than the usual propaganda pabulum put out by the Singapore Broadcasting Corporation. . . .

I decided to open the film with a quick-cut montage of vox-pop interviews. Although most people opted for safety rather than freedom of speech, we did manage to get enough comments pro and con to edit together a catchy opening to the film, topped off with my favorite—an old woman selling bean curd on the street. . . .

"Don't ask me," she quipped. "I'm just an old woman selling bean curd on the street. This is Singapore. The government decides everything. Got questions?—go ask the government. . . . In Singapore the government tells everybody what to do! Not me! You think they'll get me to live on one of those little boxes [the new government-development housing blocks] in the sky? I'll sleep here on the street."

I was so indulgently in love with it that I saved it for the last quote in our montage and used it in its entirety. Everyone loved it, or said they did. Except for the piper. The director of Singapore Broadcasting also happened to be the minister of culture. As we looked at the film, he requested a few small changes but insisted I delete my favorite seller of bean curd.

Reluctantly, I cut it down about half, using some uninspiring cutaways. The minister requested me to make a video copy and have it delivered to his office. Later I heard of his intentions. Convinced that such heresy would put this know-it-all American on the next flight out of paradise, he temporarily relinquished his editorial control to the authoritarian prime minister of Singapore . . . who I was told really liked the film. Anyway, I was not asked to reedit, and the film was given heavy advertizing and prime billing on Singapore TV.

So I was right—but so terribly wrong. Because I didn't understand the needs of my client. The minister of culture wanted safe films, innocuous films that spoon-fed the Singaporean populace with what they needed to know to understand government policy. He had no need for American-style cutting-edge films that would either put his neck on the chopping block or wind up, as this one did, making him lose a lot of face. My career at Singapore Broadcasting ended quietly at the end of my contract.

Len McClure, Singapore

Afterword

OCCASIONALLY WHILE GIVING SOME documentary courses, I've had to give exams. Apart from the usual questions on Robert Flaherty, cinema verité, and whether Leni Riefenstahl was an artist or Hitler propagandist, I usually throw in one other: "What is the difference between feature films and documentary?" Most of the answers follow the same pattern. Feature films are fiction, done in studios, with actors, and made for strict entertainment and for profit. Documentaries deal with real life, don't use actors, go in for interviews, use archives extensively, and are not shot in the studios. A few refine their answers to include a discussion of faking in documentaries, the nature of docudrama, whether documentary reaches a higher plane of truth than features, and whether Michael Moore is over the top.

What interests me most, however, is when the students start discussing how documentary purpose differs from features. "Documentary is there to inform, to educate, even to act as a rabble-rouser," one enthusiast wrote. And, of course, she was right!

In this book, I've generally refrained from discussing documentary objectives, as my purpose has been to write a short, down-to-earth guide for survival in the professional world. Yet, I know in the end, however practical the target of this book, documentary goals must be mentioned because we do believe in change, yes, we do believe in the power of documentary, and, yes, we do believe we have to bear witness.

When I was researching this book, many friends replied, often at length, to my queries. As I read and reread their responses, one set of observations by Mark Benjamin kept reverberating in my mind. Mark is a very generous friend who has helped me on a number of occasions and is also a very gifted and successful New York filmmaker. What Mark wrote is well worth repeating, as his remarks seem to me to summarize precisely what we're at and why we make documentaries.

Don't do this documentary career thing just as a job. You will not succeed. This work is all about "heart," feeling people and life. You have got to be concerned with the human condition. Documentaries have the power to make change. Change is hard, and so is making documentary films, but the cumulative power of all social political films is awesome. This career is not for the weak. My motto has always been, "We are film warriors, and God is our gaffer." We shoot till it's dark, and the amazing characters you meet making documentaries will enrich your life beyond anything you could wish for.

Index

ALAN ROSENTHAL was born in England, studied law at Oxford, and has made more than fifty films, mainly in the United States, England, and Israel. He helped train Israel Television's film staff and has written seven other books about documentary and drama, including a book of recollections about Israel, *Jerusalem, Take One! Memoirs of a Jewish Filmmaker.* He has taught at Stanford University and British, Australian, and Mexican film schools and is a professor in the Department of Communications at the Hebrew University, Jerusalem. His recent films include *The Brink of Peace* for WNET, New York; *Eichmann: The Secret Memoirs, Stalin's Last Purge* for German television; and *Waves of Freedom* for ARTE and ZDF. Another recent film, *Out of the Ashes*, won a Christopher Award and a Peabody Award for Journalism. The author is currently finishing a docudrama for French and Australian television on crime and transportation in the nineteenth century called *Condemned to the Penal Colony.*